To
Suzanne 2011
christmas
Mom

Table *Life*

SAVORING
THE HOSPITALITY
OF JESUS
IN YOUR HOME

Joanne Thompson

BEAVER'S
POND
PRESS

ISBN: 978-1-59298-453-4

Library of Congress Catalog Number: 2011939321

Book design and typesetting: Jill Blumer

Printed in the United States of America

First Printing: 2011

15   14   13   12   11   5   4   3   2   1

BEAVER'S POND
PRESS

7104 Ohms Lane, Suite 101
Edina, Minnesota 55439 USA
(952) 829-8818
www.BeaversPondPress.com

To order, visit www.BeaversPondBooks.com or call 1-800-901-3480.
Reseller and special sales discounts available.

To Jill Kristen and Shelly Anne,
you once lived at our table, and now have tables of your own.

"ONE GENERATION WILL COMMEND YOUR WORKS TO ANOTHER...
THEY WILL CELEBRATE YOUR ABUNDANT GOODNESS
AND JOYFULLY SING OF YOUR RIGHTEOUSNESS."

(Psalms 145:4, 7)

Acknowledgments

Thank you to…

The many who have prayed this project to completion. You know who you are, and God has answered your prayers.

The many friends who gave me their table stories to share. You are living it.

Jill Levin and Barbara Marshak—You made our writers' group a joyful discovery of pursuing our callings.

Dr. Harv Powers—You spoke empowering words to my heart and gave me your fine-tip pen.

Dr. Suzanne Stubblefield—College roomie, little did I know that many years later, one conversation over dinner would connect your heart to the vision of *Table Life*. You listen and bless with a grace-filled heart.

Angela Wiechmann—Your editorial expertise and genuine enthusiasm for *Table Life* was indeed the perfect provision for this novice author. I didn't know I'd have this much fun working so hard. Thanks for your amazing partnership.

Jill Blumer—You transformed text into beauty. What a touch!

Amy Quale—You guided me through the publishing maze with kind confidence

Roger—You have steadfastly believed in me. *Table Life* wouldn't exist apart from your encouragement and the life we have shared in serving three churches. After our wedding day, I left California and followed you to Denver for your seminary education; you left bland potatoes and followed my hankering for Thai curry chicken and other exotic tastes. When I think of all the friends we've made at the table, I am reminded of one of your favorite quotes: "We are rich enough!"

Author's Note

My prayer is that *Table Life* renews your love for Christ and your vision for hospitality in your home. May your table become a place for joyful connection where your children flourish, your heart grows in faith, and your community of faith is strengthened in love.

I have written *Table Life* from the comforts of a prosperous Minneapolis suburb. But throughout the world, in every nation, there are orphans waiting for a family to belong to and a table to celebrate. All profits generated from the sale of *Table Life* will be joyfully given to adoption and rescue ministries. This is my commitment first to Jesus Christ, my Redeemer, and then to you, the reader.

Contents

CHAPTER 1

Called to Table Life

Letting Jesus show us table life.

The bread store in my town is known for its irresistible hospitality. It's a simple place with rows of bread racks, an industrial mixer, and a mammoth maple wood kneading surface. Puffs of flour occasionally drift through the workroom. Customers mill around the homey space with eyes on the bread samples, such as cranberry orange, Tuscan rosemary garlic, and sunflower wheat. Oh, how I love the ritual of the sample counter. It's like coming home for dinner, knowing my favorite meal is on the table. A clerk points to each possibility with a bread knife and waits for my choice. The shocker is the size of the samples. She cuts a chunk of bread that matches the sipping time of a sixteen-ounce latte. After she slathers it with butter, I receive the gift. What delicious comfort. This welcome still amazes me. It's so free, not showy—a simple welcome that offers the nourishing pleasure of whole-grain goodness.

Christian hospitality is like a great harvest of bread, delighting us with a joy only God can supply. It's common to hear phrases like "pray by faith," "witness by faith," "give by faith." But how often have you heard someone say, "I entertain by faith"? It sounds unfamiliar, doesn't it? Our tendency is to categorize hospitality into two groups of people: those who naturally love to entertain and those who say, "That's not my thing." Both perspectives may be devoid of faith. And yet it is *faith*—that is, our living connection with God—that opens the door for every Christ follower to experience God's treasures of the table.

Hospitality is more about your faith than your competence. A farmer can't create a single grain of wheat himself, but by faith, he cooperates with God by tilling, planting, watering, and expecting a great return. Sharing your table isn't fueled by faith in your magnificent entertaining skills or gregarious personality; it's believing that God will satisfy hearts as well as appetites when you share your table in Jesus' name.

Our twenty-first-century American culture has a love affair with the goodness and art of food, and its revered teachers' classroom is the Food Network. Rachael, Emeril, Paula, Alton, Sandra, Ina, Giada. You've probably never been in their homes for dinner, but maybe you've curled up on your couch to admire their succulent sensations, gawk at their dream kitchens, and listen to them tapping their hundred-dollar knives with peppered precision. And today's DVR life allows us to watch them anytime we crave a food diversion. If you've never watched the Food Network, just think of Martha or Julia. Every generation loves its stars in the kitchen.

Think with me about these kitchen stars: Every week, millions of women and men watch the stars perform. They are an assorted lot— perky, competitive, Southern warm, demure, bombastic, intellectual, sexy. It's all part of the entertainment. They delight us with funny stories about crying while they teach us how to properly peel an onion. They're friends to many homes by enlivening the often-neglected place of the kitchen. They entertain. They are passionate, gifted teachers. They're inspiring, innovative, and so organized! I'm a "messy" in my kitchen. Always have been. Please don't look in my kitchen drawers. (I still haven't figured out how itsy food debris gathers in their corners.) I'll never entertain with the finesse of the professional foodies, but truth be said, their shows inspire, or at least woo me to veg out with effortless enjoyment. Occasionally I'll try their recipes or check their websites.

Trust me. I have no malcontent for these passionate chefs. But it's beneficial to press the pause button long enough to discern how their kitchen glitz may divert us from sharing meals in the spirit of authentic Christian hospitality. It doesn't have to, but I wonder how often it does. As viewers who live in a competitive, image-saturated culture, we are at risk of burdening ourselves with an ideal standard wrapped in the ribbon of perfectionism. The professionals aren't bad people; they just love what they do. I'm thinking about *how our minds take in the images* we see on the screen. Like the proverbial frog about to croak as it cooks in a slowly warmed pan, we don't notice how media meals might misdirect our hearts' longings away from God's table.

These chefs cook on a stage where cameramen take and retake until they get it just right. They have stagehands who arrange on a marble counter a bowl of flaming red peppers adjacent to plump Boston lettuce. Under carefully positioned floodlights, water droplets glaze tomatoes that glisten like jewels. And don't forget the staff behind the scene: a program director, producer, makeup artist, wardrobe designer, purchasing agent (wouldn't it be great to have someone do all your shopping?), and room designer.

And it's not just about the kitchen. The chefs often move toward that wonderful gathering place—the table. Hello, designer table! One day it's fun and funky. Another day it's casual cool. Some days it's so splendidly gorgeous, it burns our eyes with envy. Have you ever had the restless thought, "I'll never have a table like

We are at risk of burdening ourselves with an ideal standard wrapped in the ribbon of perfection.

that"? Creativity celebrates God, but when we allow someone else's gifts to poke holes in our own contentment, we're not likely to share the tables in our homes.

These creative cooks intuitively know the table creates a connecting place for friends and family. As they extol the virtues of the table at the close of a show, our minds are unconsciously absorbing messages: Ideal cook. Ideal resources. Ideal kitchen. Ideal table. By the way, have you ever seen an eight-year-old boy run through the kitchen while Rachael was fixing a pasta dish? Have you ever seen Martha mindlessly pour liquid gold chicken broth through a colander into the drain? We as viewers are motivated to try their recipes, but the surreal standard of showtime doesn't teach our hearts how to treasure life at the table. They offer an ideal deal, but can't produce the *real deal*.

And here lies a subtlety—we're tempted to live vicariously at their tables. We let their snazzy chefery and their homey homilies suffice as "virtual meals," and then we dash out the door to a world of stress. In reality, we can't taste their food, and in our heart of hearts, we yearn for our own tables. But we just don't seem to make it happen. I'm not blaming Hollywood for the sadness of the missing table. There are millions who don't experience life at the table who have never seen a cooking show. But our stargazing reflects our distracted, exhausted lives. How can we make our way back to the table? What *is* the real deal, anyway?

God speaks a word to us through the life of his Son, Jesus. His abundance at our tables is fresh and inviting, simple and satisfying. I call it *table life*. We experience table life as we open our hearts by faith to follow the example and teachings of Jesus; that is, how Jesus honored the table experience. When Jesus came to live on earth in pursuit of our faraway hearts, he made a beeline to the kitchen table. Once upon many meals, Jesus—the strong man on a mission to redeem the world—took time to eat dinner. Imagine the satisfied grin on his suntanned face as he ate crispy fried fish and plump pomegranate seeds. Christ lived table life not on a television stage, but in Judean homes. Jesus needed food, but his lifestyle also demonstrated a passionate preference for the table *as an expression of the kingdom.* His practice of eating meals with others in their homes was an answer to the prayer he taught his disciples, "Thy kingdom come, thy will be done on earth as it is in heaven." Over meals, he connected with family, strangers, skeptics, and friends. Across the table, hearts made for relationships came alive.

When it's all said and done, life is about God's gift of relationship. *Table Life* is a guide to help us savor the liberating presence of Christ around our tables. Get ready to receive.

✦ ✦ ✦ ✦ ✦ ✦ ✦ ✦ ✦ ✦ ✦ ✦ ✦

I stood at the sink, scrubbing flecks of dried basil out of the soup tureen as the stubborn herb seemed determined to leave an enduring tribute to table life. The September evening might have seemed a little too warm for soup and bread. A few guests probably sweated as we slurped tomato chicken soup, but I didn't notice. What I remember is the distance of busy, anonymous lives shrinking into the glad-hearted welcome of Christ's presence.

There were eight new faces at our table. We all worshiped at the same church, but had never met each other before this night. I extended the invitation over the phone, not knowing what mix of personalities would come to our table. But I've learned that when I invite by faith and let Christ be the host, I am free to live the adventure of inviting in strangers. Our conversation revealed an instant bond—we were all transplants to Minnesota. There wasn't a wild-rice native among us.

Among other surprises, Christ prepared this meal to give us a place to talk about adjustments to Midwest culture.

From the sweet drawl of Georgia to the melodic timbre of Chile, this motley group of believers spent two hours living at the table. Stories were told of a ride in a blimp, a courtship by e-mail, and wrangling a hundred head of cattle. As we passed the bread, it felt as if Christ stretched his arms around us like a father, grateful his children came home.

After years of pursuing table life, I'm convinced "the unseen guest" is constantly working. He reveals his presence as he weaves intricate details of stories at the table. This happens whenever we embrace table life. Halfway through one meal, we discovered there were three people who had identical twins. We just laughed. These three people had extremely different personalities, and yet the commonality of twin births somehow worked to draw us all into the gift of our common life in Christ. I'll never forget yet another night when, unplanned by us but orchestrated by God, three men each shared their stories of receiving Christ's forgiveness while in prison. Awe, not sherbet, was the dessert that night.

✦ ✦ ✦ ✦ ✦ ✦ ✦ ✦ ✦ ✦ ✦ ✦ ✦

Where do you live? Does your front door swing open to Lookout Mountain Drive or the numerical land of 12345 Upper 149th Street? Can you see the city lights from your fourth-floor apartment? Maybe you step down to go into a basement dwelling? Wherever you live, the Lord God has designs for your kitchen table. There's no place like home—*your* home—to experience and share his kingdom joy. And there's no place like your table to truly feel at home.

Yet we tend to be like children who groan when their mother says, "Time for dinner." Instead of anticipating the gift of a meal, we feel like dinner is an interruption to our agendas. Christ is present at our tables, waiting to serve us satisfying feasts. Our Creator knows just what we need. God, who made food for our provision and pleasure, made the table for our souls.

We are a going people. Going isn't bad. Christ said, "Go and make disciples." (Matthew 28:19) My pastor (with whom I also happen to share my popcorn bowl) often closes the worship service with the affirmation, "You go as the living church out there." But the *pace* of the world's *going* has gone mad. Before the cell phone era, a friend once told me she needed an illuminated sign on top of her van to communicate to her neighborhood friends as she zoomed up and down the street. We live in the richest nation in the world. We build the largest houses in the world. But nobody is home. Author Ken Gire writes, "We have big things—we know big things. But we don't look into each other's eyes. We're starved for a life that not only senses the sacred in the world around us but savors it. We're famished for experiences that are real and relationships that are deep." [1]

Are you famished but frustrated because you can't find your table? Do you have a stash of great recipes, but only a few memories of connection over a meal? Has your kitchen table become a monument to neglected relationships or failed good intentions? Have you made the effort to invite people to your home, but they weren't available? Did it feel like rejection? Are you worried or afraid your guests will pick up on your imperfections—tattered upholstery, bouncy kids, chipped crockery? Does the call of hospitality sound like exercise—you know it's good for you, but it just feels like it requires too much energy to make it happen?

Our Creator knows just what we need. God, who made food for our provision and pleasure, made the table for our souls.

Has the convenience of restaurant meals fostered complacency about the blessings of your own table? Restaurant meals offer convenience but often fail to provide genuine intimacy. In contrast, sharing a meal at home is inherently personal. Our tables are designed by God for the winsome grace of vulnerability.

Relax. This is not a proposal to boycott your favorite coffee shop or a mandate to make your home a twenty-four hour diner. It's an invitation to balance your going life with Christ's gifts waiting to be opened, enjoyed, and shared at home, where your feet slide under the dinner table.

The following chapters are each comprised of three sections: First, The Jesus Table retells the story of a table Jesus ate at or taught about and then suggests how his actions and words call us to pursue table life. It builds a foundation to tune our hearts to table life. This is followed by Finding Your Table and Setting Your Table. In each chapter you'll discover an "Oh, Dear" story. These are intended to remind all of us that hospitality is not about being perfect. And when those "imperfect moments" come to the fore, they are recoverable with grace and humility. Explore with me the task of finding and setting our tables.

Finding Your Table

Finding what is lost guarantees joy. You simply can't help but be happy. Jesus said, "Suppose a woman has ten silver coins and loses one. Does she not light a lamp, sweep the house and search carefully until she finds it? And when she finds it, she calls her friends and neighbors together and says, 'Rejoice with me: I have found my lost coin.'" (Luke 15:8)

Take joy! God gives every believer a life to live at the table. All we need to do is find it. Finding your table doesn't mean "looking for your table," like standing in

Has the convenience of restaurant meals fostered complacency about the blessings of your own table?

front of an open refrigerator, searching for the mustard, when it's staring back at you on the top shelf. It's not the size of a table that makes it difficult to find. Our first dinner table was a forty-gallon pickle barrel topped by plywood. A large hole in the center of the plywood crowned this less-than-lovely furniture. Its rustic style was impossible to miss in our red-shag, one-bedroom apartment. But only time would tell whether its presence and purpose would be ignored or honored.

Instead, the act of finding our tables calls us to search our hearts. It's a lifestyle check, a heart check. I'm convinced we walk past our tables without regard for their significance and meaning because of the pressures of our culture and the idols of our hearts. *Finding the table* happens when with Jesus' help we identify the pressures and topple the idols. Distractions are everywhere. But remember, finding your table is worth the search. It's the place where mouths and hearts receive more gifts from Jesus.

Setting Your Table

Jesus said it is good to be like a child. When the disciples asked about greatness in the kingdom, Jesus motioned a child to come close. The pint-size presence made the teacher's point—humility paves the way of the kingdom. We need to let a child show us how to set our tables. It sounds dangerous, but it's liberating.

Our daughters, Jill and Shelly, began setting the table as toddlers. By that time, we had replaced the pickle barrel with a pine trestle table and benches (now covered with cracked varnish and polished memories). They climbed on the bench without a clue that the knife goes on the right and the fork on the left. Their puffy pink hands let go of the flatware like hot potatoes, but above the clang rang pure love. They were glad and proud, and so was I. I wasn't delighting over their mastery of a perfectly set table. That wasn't the goal. I was delighting in their wholehearted participation and expectation of the table. We did it together. My joy in doing this work with my daughters captures God's father-heart toward us.

To set your table is to do hospitality with God. It is to take the practical steps that reflect *attitudes* and *habits* growing out of your faith relationship with God. Faith fuels great expectations—not demands, but anticipation. Faith lives in teachable hearts ready to receive his gifts at a meal. As we allow Christ to connect the dots between our grocery list and the conversations around the table, we grow with a childlike heart. Setting the table by faith isn't just about what we do; it shapes who we become.

Setting the table by faith isn't just what we do; it shapes who we become.

✦ ✦ ✦ ✦ ✦ ✦ ✦ ✦ ✦ ✦ ✦ ✦ ✦

Whatever our tables are made of—Formica, plywood, oak, or exotic hardwood from Tanzania—what matters is how we *view* them. When we look with eyes informed by the practice of the New Testament Jewish home, we discover the stunning simplicity that the table served as an altar. This perspective infuses meaning to the tables of our twenty-first-century homes.

In the Old Testament, an altar—made of rock, usually flat—was something the Israelites *came* to by faith. Coming to the altar was intentional. As they offered sacrifices, they received forgiveness for sin. The altar was the place to receive the divine blessing of God's forgiveness and mercy. The burden of sin—envy, pride, gossip—transferred to the animal sacrifice as they opened their hearts to God in confession. The altar meant hope and renewal. When the Temple was destroyed, a shift occurred: The family table was the only place to gather. Families listened to fathers read the Torah, they confessed sin, and they ate in a spirit of celebration and gratitude. Once Christ's death fulfilled God's permanent provision for sin, believers understood that an altar for sin sacrifice was no longer needed. But *viewing* the table as an altar remained imprinted in the imagination of the Jewish believer. In the new order of Christ, faith remakes us to be a people who treasure table life.

When a resistant two-year-old refuses to eat his meat loaf, then Mom squeezes ketchup on his plate, what happens? A miracle! Can taking time to share a peanut-butter sandwich produce heart change? Test it! Be attentive and watch what God will do. Don't try to understand the mystery. Just enjoy the meal. Experience the everyday miracle of Christ at your table. "Build altars in places where I remind you who I am, and I will come and bless you there." (Exodus 20:24, *NLT*)

CHAPTER 2

Thanks for Supper, Mom!

Jesus the boy comes to his parents' table.

The Jesus Table

Years before Jesus blessed bread to feed a crowd of five thousand on the Galilean hillside, he broke bread at home as a boy in his parents' house. Christ's journey to the table began when he left heaven to be born in Bethlehem (which means "the house of bread"). Birthed in the womb of time, Jesus woke up hungry to every sunrise.

Jesus, who made the universe and who waters the earth and decks the valleys with grain, still needed to eat his oatmeal as a child! He didn't theologize about dinner; he ate dinner. He bit into plump grapes, licked honey off his sticky fingers, and chewed savory roasted lamb. I wonder if his tummy growled when he listened to Joseph teach from the Torah about the land flowing with milk and honey—the barley, almonds, raisins, cucumbers, melons, onion, garlic, pomegranates, and lentils. One thing we know for sure: He took time to eat.

Scripture says of Jesus that as a child "he grew and became strong; he was filled with wisdom, and the grace of God was upon him." (Luke 2:40) Jesus grew because every day he sat at the table provided by Mary and Joseph. God the Father's eternal plan was for Jesus to be born among the Jewish people, who practiced a cohesive table tradition. His parents taught him how to properly eat with his fingers (no forks in his day) and pass the lentils to his brothers. When Mary called Jesus for dinner, he bolted home just like any Middle Eastern boy—with an empty tummy and sweaty forehead baked by the searing sun. His thirst and cravings signaled that dinner couldn't be served too soon. Mary no doubt smiled the first time Jesus learned to say, "Thanks, Mom. That was good. May I have more?" Even the Son of God needed to learn manners, but eating meals was more than just a lesson in manners and a fuel-up stop.

Every day, Jesus lived life at the table. Mealtime provided wholeness for his body and soul. At the table, the boy Jesus received eye contact and focused attention from Mom and Dad. I've often wondered how his personality expressed itself. Was he a lively talker, or a wide-eyed listener? That answer is locked in his family history, but there's no doubt he learned an intentional mealtime rhythm from his parents and faith community. At the table, Jesus heard the timbre of Joseph's voice offer a prayer, read scripture, tell stories. Jesus celebrated feasts with his family, and his peasant home buzzed with the weekly preparations for the Sabbath meal. On the night before Passover, he searched like a scout for hidden leaven. Eating meals with family and friends, conversation, laughter, and a faith-oriented focus was ordinary life for the boy Jesus.

Meals provided the time and space, rhythm and pace, where Jesus grew in favor with God the Father as well as with his earthly family. He left his Father's heaven, but not his Father's heart. We can't unpack the mysteries of how the child Son of God developed. But we can confidently assert that every toss of grapes into his mouth sparked gratitude for his Father's provision. Jesus ate dinner conscious of his Father's glad presence. Faith infused Jesus with a secure, joyful knowing that his Father, the giver of every good and perfect gift, was home.

So what do we learn from the boy Jesus? I can almost hear your thoughts: "Okay, all I need is a perfect child, and just maybe life at the table will happen." We are not exactly like Jesus, but he chose to become like us. The Father could have delivered Jesus to this earth with a body not needing food. It doesn't sound like a pleasurable way to live, but wouldn't it have been more efficient for the kingdom if Jesus never had to *take time* to eat a meal?

Don't miss the meaning of Jesus stepping down from eternity to eat his oatmeal. His choosing to come to the table sets the record straight: Mealtime is sacred. A meal is not a church service, but the table remains an altar. It's the centerpiece of family life. Mealtime is set apart as an enduring expression of God's kingdom provision, "Give us this day our daily bread." Time is God's good creation, and mealtime is God's metronome designed to bind our busy lives to the Father. This is the life the boy in Nazareth lived.

Finding Your Table

Hospitality within the church family begins with treasuring table life with our own family—our sons and daughters, mothers and fathers, husbands and wives. We know it matters, but sometimes we lose our way. One of the secret scars of some adults now raising children is that they have only painful, stress-laden memories of meals. Janet tells her story.

> *Our family shared a rectangular table seating seven. My emotionally disconnected father sat at one end, reading his* Field & Stream *magazine. My older brother sat to his left. My brother's job was to make sure a buttered piece of bread was always on Dad's plate, so Dad would not have any interruptions to his solitary dining. If*

Time is God's good creation, and mealtime is God's metronome designed to bind our busy lives to the Father.

the bread was not ready, my brother got a painful flick on the head. I remember tears running down my brother's reddened face.

Mom tried to keep the four of us as quiet as possible so Dad could "eat in peace." My deaf grandmother also lived with us, and sometimes her teeth made a clacking sound. This infuriated Dad, so sometimes he'd leave the table, taking his plate to the kitchen. This was our daily dinner scene.

Sometimes the stress got so high, I couldn't eat much. Other times, I finished my meal as soon as I could and then ran over to my girlfriend's house. Her alcoholic parents would always feed me well, if they weren't in one of their drunken fights.

Looking back, I realize our table repeated history from the past. My father's father, a young widower, would leave a few opened cans of beans or peas on the table for the five kids while he went off to the local bar to drink his pain away.

Christ came to the table and completed his earthly mission to provide hope and healing for every family. Sometimes our hurts motivate us to raise our families differently. But unhealed wounds often paralyze the heart and will. If the table of your childhood produced shame instead of a haven of love, you may feel trapped by the paradox of longing for the table yet also fearing what it signified in your childhood. But Jesus invites you to view your table as a place to open your heart to God's grace so you can write a new story in your home. The table calls your heart to hope.

Maybe your table hasn't been a war zone, but is it a comfort zone? Has the speed of life stripped the gears of God's mealtime metronome? Did yesterday's sip of fresh orange juice squeeze a sweet pause of praise from your lips? Or have you forgotten about sipping entirely? Hurried meals harm us more than we realize. They dishonor the image of God in us. Pets lap their bowls and leave; people are to receive food in the fellowship of communal life.

As comparison, consider another family ritual—the giving and receiving of gifts at Christmas. We're entertained when a two-year-old rips open a gift, looks at it for five seconds, then hastily grabs another. But I've noticed, even with such innocent madness, a slight ache rises in the soul of the giver, for this is not how gifts ought to be received! Yet this is the way culture lures us away from the table. Eat and run. Eat on the run. Eat fast food, fast. Eat alone. Eat in the van. Eat in front of the computer. Eat in shifts. Eat whenever. Many families do eat together in some fashion, some of the time. But even then, it is how we eat together that threatens home. We have time to stuff a burger in our mouths, but that's about all.

What's fueling this run past the table? In the book *Putting Families First*, William J. Doherty, PhD, and Barbara Z. Carlson describe the morphing values of American culture in the twenty-first century: "We believe that the adult world of hyper-competition and marketplace values has invaded the family. We are raising children in a culture that defines a good parent as an opportunity provider in a competitive world."[1] Is your identity as a parent shamed by the fangs of "hyper-competition and marketplace values"? Are you tempted to believe your children's well-being and future hinge primarily on performance and competition? These cultural allurements often steal the dinner hour from house and home as basketball practice, piano lessons, and math tutoring go well into the evening. But a commitment to table life empowers you to look at your children's future with eyes of discerning love today.

Years ago, I scribbled on a scrap of paper, "My home is the only place I can control." My words weren't the strategy of a control-freak mother poised to lock her daughters in the house. They formed a prayer that brought focus and freedom. I agreed with God that my primary sphere of influence was in the home. As a

Gratitude is as essential to our children's emotional happiness as food is to their physical strength

parent, I was feeling discouraged by the pervasive influence of secular culture. I couldn't control the foul language my children heard or the promiscuity of media. I couldn't change escalating expectations of suburban leisure. The world's values are not like the tides that come and go; they're more like an uncontained fire hydrant that indiscriminately blasts water onto our streets. The cultural floods will always surge. But God gives the believer an ark called home.

Let the durable image of the ark speak to you about God's passion for your home. Noah's family didn't need a crystal chandelier to survive. As the family leader, Noah needed to believe God about his design for a refuge. So by faith, he hammered day by day for a hundred years. The storms came, God kept his promises, and the family eventually dined under the rainbow. Parents, believe God's design. Trust him. Don't allow the clamor of culture to rob your family of real life.

What do you treasure? When it's all said and done, what's of great worth to you? Jesus said, "Where your treasure is, there will your heart be also." (Matthew 6:21) Has your heart lost connection with the ritual of family meals? We have many routines. Routines are necessary—they organize days, make us efficient, and give our minds a break. But it's relational rituals, such as mealtime, that create emotional connection.

If you tend to be a "gulp-and-go" family, it will require patience, wisdom, and an honest look at your heart to recalibrate a healthy family rhythm. Don't demand a seven-day legalism. Lift your sight to the law of love. Help yourself find your table by kindly considering the following questions:

* How many days a week does your family spend thirty minutes or more eating dinner together (without interference from the TV, computer, or cell phone)?

* Every yes means a no to something else. What do you want your family to say yes to? Discuss with your spouse or wise friend what your yes will require you to say no to.

* What legacy treasures from the table do you want to give your children? Do you have a favorite table memory from your childhood? Luxuriate in the gift. Talk about it at dinner tonight.

* Have you asked God for help? If your childhood family meals were chaotic, hurtful, or absent, ask God to heal the wounds and give you strength to create a new table life legacy. Invite yourself to dinner with a family who values life around the table. Learn from their lifestyle; receive the hope of the table.

Lifestyle Check: Does my family sit at or race past the table?

Heart Check: In what way have my decisions about family table life been swayed by how culture defines a good parent as an opportunity provider?

Setting Your Table

Whenever we join God, he changes us. As parents make mealtime a priority, we create a setting designed by God to foster gratitude. Gratitude is as essential to our children's emotional happiness as food is to their physical strength. Setting the table by faith is not just showing up for a five-minute fuel-up; it is cultivating a humble awareness that we are receiving a gift. It is eating with gratitude. Imagine your family hearing the prayer of this African Christian after eating dinner:

We thank you, Lord; that was such a good meal. The soup was good. The meat was good. The hot pepper and the yam were good. O Lord, our stomachs are full.

Did You Know?

"A large national study of American teenagers found a strong link between regular family meals and a wide range of positive outcomes: academic success, psychological adjustment, and lower rates of alcohol use, drug use, early sexual behavior, and suicidal risk. On the flip side, not having regular family meals was associated with higher risks in all those areas." [2]

Our bodies have what they need. This is a new miracle every day. We thank you for it and also for the good taste that lingers on our tongues. How refreshing your water was! With this meal, you gave us the strength required for the day. Add to it your Spirit so that we might use your strength rightly. Give us, besides food for our bodies, your heavenly food for our whole life. Praised be you, merciful God. Amen.[3]

I've imagined my grandchildren's assorted responses if they had listened to someone with such a grateful heart. They would be peeking at the one praying, fidgeting with fascination at the name of every food, smiling at the guest's contagious happiness, or maybe saying the "amen" right along with him. But the true blessing is that each of their porous souls would drink in gratitude.

We all have times when we bring grumpiness to the table. The arsenic hour of low blood sugar and fatigue haunts every home. The table ought to be a safe place to come as we are, famished and funky, but with an uncompromised commitment that it's the place where we choose to disengage from the entangling threads of the outside world. At the table, children are invited to taste, hear, and learn to live everyday gratitude.

Unfortunately, life's rat race blinds adults from the wonder that we are receiving a gift every time we eat. We want our children to be grateful, but we lose this center ourselves. In *The Meaning of Gifts*, Paul Tournier writes, "Gifts have many meanings, deep and subtle, both for those who give and those who receive."[4] I know from experience finding or making just the right gift gives me joy. When was the last time you thought of God's happiness as he provided guacamole for your burrito? Then there's God's gift of time at the table; it's as pure as white linen. Time is as precious as food itself. Not just because of its scarcity, but because of its meaning. Spending time munching and sharing a cup of sunflower seeds is a little thing (unless you haven't eaten for days), but that "little thing" is soul-significant as it awakens gratitude to God.

Gratitude isn't a Pollyanna life; it's a pilgrim life of the true self we're created to be. I've noticed I like being around people who open up their hearts in gratitude. It's so refreshing, I wonder why we don't do it more often. It softens disappointments and struggles and invites me to reorient my heart to God. At the close of an evening with a friend, she casually said, "It's amazing what can happen over a cup of coffee." A blooming blade of gratitude poked through, and I feel more alive remembering her open heart. Day by day, gratitude changes people, families, and churches.

King Solomon often mused on family life. When I read his words, "Better is a dry morsel with quiet than a house full of feasting with strife" (Proverbs 17:1), my intuition tells me he had some challenging mealtimes at home. But his life passion was to apply wisdom to every circumstance. "By wisdom a house is built, by knowledge its rooms are filled with rare and beautiful treasures." (Proverbs 24:3–4) When done in faith, the following practical steps and heart habits will fill your home with rare and beautiful treasures.

1. *Build your family circle, again and again.* This is every parent's responsibility. No one else will do it for you. The family circle is a permeable boundary that prioritizes the rhythm of coming and sitting down, face to face. God knows sitting is a necessary posture for us. When we sit at the table, we position ourselves to receive, rest, and relate. In Deuteronomy 6, God commands parents to practice the sitting-down moments of life for the sake of love—loving God and loving each other. So, be countercultural: Don't plan meals around activities; plan activities around your meals. Before your family calendar gets colored in by multitasking

Nutritional counselors recommend that parents decide the "when," "what," and "where" of the meal; children decide the "how much." Family meals minimize the likelihood of eating disorders and maximize the opportunity for balanced nutrition. Maintain the integrity of your circle by resisting the temptation of habitually eating meals in the van. I recommend The Surprising Power of Family Meals *by Miriam Weinstein.*

agendas that scatter your clan, color in a few special meals to win hearts for home. Make a sound check inside your circle. Turn off all technology that distracts from the goodness of listening and talking to one another.

2. *Serve gratitude.* Jesus always gave thanks. It's an intriguing reminder, since he created all food. But for Jesus, food was pure blessing, neither feared nor abused. As your table becomes an altar in *your* eyes, you will create a home defined by the wholesome spirit of moderation, celebration, and sanctification. These three table values from our Judeo-Christian roots produce the rewards of physical, emotional, and spiritual health in our families. Engage in the wonder that you are receiving a gift when you eat (and prepare and serve) a meal. Don't let the moods your child brings to the table define your happiness. Parents are the grownups who can choose to overcome daily difficulties with the self-discipline of gratitude. Guard mealtime from the landmines of criticism and complaint. Discipline children elsewhere. Make a habit of weaving gratitude into your conversations. Tell your children what you appreciate about each of them. Tell a story of how you experienced God in your day. Here's a power-packed nutrient for your children: Use the table as a time to verbally express love and respect to your spouse. Your eavesdropping children will grow like daisies in a greenhouse, even if they don't eat all their vegetables.

3. *Cherish Sundays.* Use your table to teach your children that your day of worship is set apart from the rest of the week. Believers celebrate the Resurrection not just on Easter, but on every Lord's Day. We are resurrection people, and what better way to celebrate than with a meal. Resist the tug to grab drive-through food after church as you head off for a Sunday packed with events. At least, make fast meals the exception, not the norm, on Sundays.

Instead of speeding up after worship, why not slow down at your table? Make your main meal a sequel to worship. It is a little, yet magnificent, adjustment to distinguish the Lord's Day in your home. Once I had three children and their mom over for a meal after church, when the word *dinner* slipped out of my mouth. The kindergartner said, "This isn't dinner, it's lunch." I didn't debate her by asking if she normally ate shish kebabs for lunch, but I told her eating "dinner" at noon was a way the Thompson home makes Sunday special. It's different from every other day of the week.

4. *Welcome creativity.* We can't create a miracle meal like Jesus, but we can appreciate his disposition. Jesus delighted in meals. He looked for the light in the eyes of those with whom he ate. My guess is that his pulse quickened as he anticipated the first sips of his miracle wine at the wedding meal in Cana.

Mimic Christ's purposefulness in giving gifts at mealtime by coming up with creative ways to enjoy your table time. Buy a "You Are Special" plate and watch your nine-year-old son sit upright when he sees it set at *his* place. You'll find more fun ideas at puttingfamilyfirst.org. Or invest in "The Original Dinner Games" by FamilyTimeFun. Years ago, our girls and their cousins Rebecca and David had a *Little House on the Prairie* Day. The entire day was centered on the preparation and eating of the meal. We had one rule: Electrical power was forbidden. The kids cooked spaghetti on the wood-burning stove. Rule violators were to be rewarded with a cream pie in the face, and Aunt Karen got it good for using her hair dryer as she freshened up before supper. This meal was so memorable, our daughter Shelly wrote about it at school. This is just an example to get you thinking about what might uniquely fit your family. Simple ideas, such as a grilled cheese sandwich candlelight dinner, also work great. Bottom line, create fun with meals.

Oh Dear!

Our plans for hosting a family of six included a picnic on the patio—hamburgers, hot dogs, baked beans, salad, brownies, and plastic plates, cups, and utensils. All went well until it started pouring rain. (I mean pouring!*) So we did the only logical thing—we brought it all inside, spread out the plastic tablecloth on the living room floor, sat down, and had an indoor picnic, pretending we were by a stream in the mountains on a gorgeous sunny day. The girls loved it and talked about it for months!*
—Judy

5. *Learn to ask honoring questions.* Jesus often asked the simplest questions to create a connection to the heart. While preparing breakfast over a charcoal fire, Jesus asked the distraught disciples, "Have you caught any fish?" (John 21:5) His question worked like a fishing line that drew Peter to shore for an intimate encounter with forgiveness and restoration. Fried fish must have never tasted better to Peter than on that misty morning.

I've learned from experience that neither children nor a husband welcome a barrage of questions at the table. Grilling like a prosecutor never creates connection. We need a gracious curiosity that invites, not demands, a response. Children feel overwhelmed by general questions like, "How was your day?" Instead, ask specific questions like, "Whom did you play with during recess today?" When children learn to tell stories—most importantly, their stories—they gain a life skill that empowers them to *feel* their value. They will reenter the shame-based world with an upright posture of wholesome self-esteem. Bedtime storytelling creates a benediction; mealtime storytelling creates a family who listens and cares. If your family has one "Queen of Verbosity" and another "Silent Sam," your table serves as the place for your children to learn (through your example) how to value and appreciate the spangled differences of human personality. You will discover helpful questions in *Keep Talking: Daily Conversation Starters for the Family Meal*, by Maureen Treacy Lahr and Julie Pfitzinger.

6. *Do it together.* Jesus was one with the Father. This union sourced the power and strength of his earthly ministry. If you are a two-parent family, begin to dialogue as a couple about the treasure factor (what you value) and the needs of your family. Oneness in your marriage will empower you to stand firm against culture's pull away from the table. For the proposals or changes on which you

agree, give them time, be flexible, and expect good things as you lead your family.

If you are a single parent, God's table plan still works. In *Putting Families First*, Dr. Doherty writes, "Whether you are a residential or nonresidential single parent, making family life the priority requires seeing yourself as a real family and acting like one in the time you have together."[5] He encourages the single parent to maintain continuity with rituals that still work, to modify rituals that don't work, or to create new ones. Perhaps one of your new rituals can be getting your children involved with meal preparation. Trust your Heavenly Father that your children will be anchored in love and develop a heart of gratitude because you honor the family ritual of a meal together.

7. Remember the dividends of a good habit. For every "Janet's story" of an abusive father's frightening antics at dinner, there are many homes waging peace at the table. Good-willed parents push through fatigue and pressure. They cast their burdens of the day on the Lord before walking through the front door so they can "practice the presence" of the family. They do the unglamorous work of digging out forks stuck in the dishwasher basket and cutting up finger food for the snot-nosed boy in the highchair. The kitchen table represents thousands of acts of nurturing love. The following story from my friend Jenny, mother of four boys, illustrates how the little things can make a big difference.

Two nights ago, I was setting food on the table for us to eat as a family, and on a whim, I pulled out candles and lit them. The boys were delighted and asked to turn off all the lights and close the blinds so we would have only the light from the candles. It was a lovely, soft atmosphere, and they were soon hugging each other and giggling. They were enjoying each other and we them. Since I am task-structure oriented, I normally don't think about the little touches, nor do I look at meals as social time (except when guests are present). Needless to say, we lit candles last night, and again (unprompted) the boys were hugging and enjoying each other around the table. I hope I have stumbled onto something that brings the joy of table time back into our home. It had gotten lost in the midst of rigorous daily life and the din of six voices all wanting to be helped or heard around the table.

So simple! A lit candle. Within the Jewish faith, the mother is assigned a specific role at the Sabbath meal: She lights two candles. No one is to snuff them prematurely; the candles burn until the wicks are gone. Moms partner with God to remind the family that the blessing of the Sabbath dinner is to be enjoyed fully.

✦ ✦ ✦ ✦ ✦ ✦ ✦ ✦ ✦ ✦ ✦ ✦ ✦

Hanging above the fireplace in our home is a cranberry-colored turkey platter with an outdoor scene of the first Thanksgiving Day—a Native American lugs a turkey over his shoulder, baskets overflow with corn and squash, Pilgrims prepare a table for the feast, and a boy sits on a log as he watches the table being set. The artist Homer Laughlin named the design "Bountiful Harvest." My mother bought this platter in 1954 with a $25 gift she received from her mother. In today's collector's market, it's worth several hundred dollars, but to me, it's a priceless symbol of my parents' holy habit of saying yes to the table. In between our luscious Thanksgiving dinners—when twenty-five-pound birds oozed yummy drippings onto the platter each year—Mom faithfully served modest meals. Godly habits grow a godly destiny.

Your household is uniquely defined by size, commitments, and season of life. Even Mary, the mother of Jesus, had her turn at washing her son's messy face and sweeping up the ancient version of Cheerios. If your family regularly eats dinner together, you are in the minority; but perhaps that significance fades into the fatigue of raising little ones or the dullness of an unexamined routine. If your family rarely eats together, there is hope for a change. For all of us, the family dinner is built on the humble recognition that God gave parents the responsibility to create the context for children to thrive.

Taste and See

It's easy to stay in a rut with meal planning. Occasionally surprise your family with a "just dessert" dinner. I knew I had stumbled upon a great idea when I surprised our girls with the one-entrée meal of strawberry shortcake. A bowl mounded with juicy strawberries welcome them to the table, and we had free reign with the whipped cream dispenser. While it was uncharacteristic of my health-food preference for a balance of protein and carbs, it fostered a happy meal (without the greasy burgers, fries, and packaging)! Try this variation.

Pizzazz Strawberries

Fresh strawberries
Balsamic vinegar
Fresh pepper

Wash and slice strawberries. Drizzle balsamic vinegar. Grind just a touch of fresh pepper over berries. Toss lightly and let soak at least 2 hours.

"Gratitude can turn a meal into a feast, a house into a home, a stranger into a friend."[6]

Super Shortcake

2 cups flour
4 teaspoons Rumford Baking Powder
½ teaspoon salt
3 tablespoons sugar
3 tablespoons butter or coconut oil
⅔ cup milk
1 egg yolk, well beaten
¼ teaspoon crushed cardamon

Combine dry ingredients in bowl. Add butter, and cut into dry mix. Mix in milk and egg yolk just until moist. Knead 4 or 5 times very lightly and pat into ⅓-inch thickness. Cut out circle shapes. Bake 10–15 minutes at 425 degrees, or until golden brown.

(Note: Most baking powders have aluminum sulfate, which can add a peculiar aftertaste. Rumford Baking Powder is aluminum free. It's worth the extra few cents!)

Daily Bread

"Don't let the world around you squeeze you into its own mould, but let God re-mould your minds from within, so that you may prove in practice that the plan of God for you is good, meets all his demands and moves towards the goal of true maturity." (Romans 12:2, *Phillips*)

Prayer

Father, thank you for mealtime. My family can't live without it. Calm the chaos. Forgive me for living carelessly without thought of the time and space where love and gratitude grow. Slow me down and satisfy me with your gifts at the table. In Jesus' name, amen.

Altar Call

Savoring the presence of Jesus at your table creates a heart of gratitude.

CHAPTER 3

A Timely Invitation

Jesus the rabbi needs friends to dine with.

"AFTER LEAVING THE SYNAGOGUE THAT DAY, JESUS WENT TO SIMON'S HOME."

(Luke 4:38, *NLT*)

The Jesus Table

On a Sabbath morning in Capernaum, the congregation crowds in the synagogue to hear the guest teacher, Jesus. They are a motley group. Robed rabbis stare with an air of distinction as they weigh every word Jesus speaks. Fishermen famished for spiritual food listen with curiosity. And in the shadows of the crowd hides a disheveled man possessed by an evil spirit. Soon trouble breaks out. From the depths of hell, the evil spirit belts a terrifying scream at Jesus. Christ steps forward, looks into the eyes of the deranged man, rebukes the evil spirit, and instantly defeats the foaming taunts of evil. His words are like the first day of creation when God spoke light into darkness and beauty into chaos. The crowd is hushed in the presence of holiness.

After the worship service, Jesus walks with Peter, Andrew, James, and John to Peter's mother-in-law's house. This day is like no other, going from a tumultuous miracle to a meal. Who talks, who listens? Do they pump Jesus with questions, or do they gush with hyperenergy among themselves while Jesus silently walks?

There's always room for Jesus at this house, a large family dwelling built to hold a crew of relatives. The central kitchen with an open-sky ceiling is surrounded by tiny bedrooms. They arrive and find Peter's mother-in-law lying flat on her bed, drenched in the grip of a raging fever. Jesus stands at her bedside, places his hand on her forehead, and raises her up; instantly, the fire leaves her body.

Imagine her first hazeless glance at Jesus, her eyes glistening with gratitude. Imagine her second look, this time with the knowing eyes of a mother. Jesus looks hungry! Eager to serve her healer, she prepares a meal and lights the lamps. Her happiness patters around the kitchen as the five believers from Capernaum recline at the table with Jesus until sundown. This day has been like no other, yet the habit of the Sabbath meal is not forgotten. Jesus needs this meal. He "lives in the moment," undistracted by his future responsibilities and previous activities. He breaks bread with his friends. His choice to linger around a meal provides his friends the reminder of how to be strengthened in faith—the afterglow of shared meals matter. Like the first visible star brings light to the twilight sky, God's work accomplished on this Sabbath day brings glory into the dining room. And the fever in the woman's body is transformed into a fire in her soul, later kindling the welcome of the first house church of the Christian faith.

✦ ✦ ✦ ✦ ✦ ✦ ✦ ✦ ✦ ✦ ✦ ✦ ✦

Jesus was a man on the move. He mingled with crowds in the synagogue and on the hillside. He never made a judgment that the crowd was a superficial, annoying waste of time. Tears salted his face as he rubbed shoulders with strangers. Yet to fulfill his Father's will, he left the crowd to gather with a few at home. Even with his divinity, he still needed to find a human rhythm. He needed rest from the crowds that swarmed around him like bees. This wasn't easy, though. Judean homes were constructed with open areas facing the street. It would be as if your house had no locked door, lawn, or driveway. The only thing separating the house from the stranger on the street was a hanging piece of cotton fabric and a few dusty steps. When people discovered Jesus in the neighborhood, they often crowded in unannounced.

But most of the time, it was Jesus' habit to eat with a few, usually in a home. I wonder what caught his attention as he stepped inside. We all have first impressions. Was it the aromatic promise of dinner? Maybe his carpenter eyes admired the sturdy lintel framing the door. Maybe he looked for a cushion to rest his feet. When he came to a home for dinner, he brought all of himself. His physical presence embodied his ongoing work as the Son of God. When Christ walked through the front door into the intimate setting of home, the pleasure of doing his Father's will and his need for a meal fit together like two puzzle pieces. Dinner on that Sabbath afternoon at Peter's mother-in-law's house was as kingdom significant as the victory of the banished evil spirit in the synagogue.

The footprints of Jesus always take us to divine appointments. Because of the homes Jesus visited, we have glimpses into transformed lives—Zacchaeus, Matthew the tax collector, Lazarus, Mary, Cleopas, and even pouting Pharisees. (We'll learn more about these transformed lives later in the book.) Jesus treasured the intimate setting of home as a place of transformation. And as a gifted storyteller, he often made a table the centerpiece of his stories. His carpenter hands likely did not build furniture, but every day he built a table with his presence. The way Jesus lived shows us that if today he walked out of the church building with the crowd or stood at the bus stop, he might wonder if you'd invite him home for dinner.

He redeemed the time by slowing down.

Finding Your Table

When was the last time you relished a timely invitation? Imagine the Capernaum meal taking place in your home. Christ's table life invites you to linger at the table with believers. That day, Jesus performed two miracles, but he also practiced a healthy habit. He made the choice to be *interdependent* by humbly receiving a meal prepared by another. In God's kingdom, the mundane and the majestic live together. Jesus the Messiah came to serve, yet at this meal he gladly let Peter's mother-in-law serve him. This meal is a reminder of how Jesus lived. He embraced his humanity by acknowledging his needs for a meal and taking time to be with his friends. He didn't strut his divinity to the table like a proud man demanding attention for his great deeds of the day. He simply relaxed, received hospitality, enjoyed table conversation, and ate a fine meal. He redeemed the time by slowing down.

We must not let the miracles keep us from seeing the Master's choice. Jesus had once fed thousands from two crusty loaves of barley bread. So we know he could have gone to a Judean cave (men do like their caves) to speak a lavish Mediterranean meal onto a platter just for himself. But he made another choice— having dinner in community.

Interdependence is a vanishing jewel in twenty-first-century culture. Our competitive, performance-oriented culture and the tyranny of the urgent woo us to *independence* and self-reliance. "I" takes precedence over "we," or a fear of inadequacy coaxes us to eat at the table by ourselves. Like too much cayenne pepper dumped in a pot of stew, these attitudes will lead to a parched soul.

I wonder if we have substituted the communal life of the table for playing on sporting teams, working on group projects, cheering with the crowd in the stands, and joining a Pilates class at the gym. These group activities are fine, but if they steal time and attention away from the simple life of breaking bread together, then we forfeit the rewards of the interdependent life designed by God to strengthen us in love. Most group activities drive toward objective, measureable goals—winning a trophy, completing a project, flattening a tummy. Table life is about love. We can't measure love, but we can experience love as we choose by faith the interdependent life, as Jesus did. Every time we follow Christ's way to the table, love grows.

Jesus has dinner in Capernaum many times; it is his ordinary, everyday interdependent table life. But it is in Jerusalem on the night before his Crucifixion that he meets his disciples for one last meal. This Passover meal is his timely invitation to express love and announce his impending death. He takes the cup and the bread, but there is no lamb on the table, for he, the Lamb of God, is sitting at the table. In the context of the meal, amidst foot washing and bickering disciples, Jesus focuses on the power of the cross. The cross provides forgiveness, defeats Satan, and *creates a new loving community.*

Jesus speaks two words at this meal that summarize the interdependent life: *one another.* He says, "Now that I, your Lord and teacher, have washed your feet, you also should wash one another's feet. I have set you an example that you should do as I have done for you" (John 13:15). This sequence fascinates me. Jesus speaks these words *after having returned to his place at the table.* From the tenderness of the towel to the devoted counsel at the table, Jesus gives to the disciples the Spirit-life of *one-anothering.*

After Judas left the meal in betrayal (fleeing table life), Jesus immediately commends one-anothering again. "A new commandment I give you: Love one another. As I have loved you, so you must love one another. By this all men will know that you are my disciples, if you love one another" (John 13:34–35). *One another*—these two words spoken by Jesus at the table break open a theme that flows throughout the New Testament. The mark of the Christian community is interdependent love.

Lifestyle Check: Do I make it a practice to open my front door to others?

Heart Check: What do I tend to value more—interdependence or independence?

Setting Your Table

Christians have a call from Jesus to connect the public places of work and worship with the private space of home. The apostle Paul wrote to the church at Rome, "Get into the practice of inviting guests home for dinner" (Romans 12:13b, *NLT*). This isn't a plea for ancient communal living or first-century Galilean house design. Author Edith Schaeffer gives a healthy perspective: "A family is a door that has hinges and a lock. The hinges should be well oiled to swing the door open during certain times, but the lock should be firm enough to let people know that the family needs to be alone part of the time, just to be a family."[1]

Perhaps you need permission to discover "just being family" is just glorious. It's the interdependent life in its original form. Don't let misguided loyalty about endless ministry needs rob you of "just family" time together. Interdependence never means taking responsibility for everyone in the crowd; that's God's job. For our family, Sundays aren't the best time to open our front door. Preaching drains Roger's introvert tank below empty. When our friends Mary and Jon invite us over after church, they know Roger's need: a wee-little conversation, a little casserole, and a lot of couch.

Interdependence implies a reciprocal life. Which is harder for you—giving or receiving? Maybe you've wandered in the crowd at church for years, wondering if

---

Did You Know?

It takes twenty minutes for your body to complete the signal from your stomach to your brain that you are full. That's why it's better to savor instead of hurriedly stuff. This physiological "law" God created supports healthy relationships—lingering at the table.

someone might invite you to dinner or if someone might accept an invite to your own home. Was it an ache or a fleeting whisper? If you've never given it a thought, you may be suffering from an acute case of independence. God is our Father. As children in his family, we really do need each other. This is where the table as an altar reveals its transforming beauty. Coming to the table is not just thinking, "I need food." It is also living, "I need *you*." It is eating with humility. Every believer's table provides an opportunity to grow in the likeness of Christ, grow in the grace of humility.

To follow Christ's movement to the table, begin by exploring which is harder for you—giving or receiving. What side of the table must you learn to come to? Healthy interdependence gives as well as receives. Usually one tends to be more developed than the other, so let's take a closer look at the two sides of the table.

The "it's-harder-to-give" types often aren't stingy with good intentions or heartfelt desires, but rather, they feel paralyzed by self-doubt. These timid folks think they have nothing to give. Self-talk rings the heavy theme of unworthiness: "They wouldn't want to come to my apartment. They don't know me. What would we talk about?" They don't trust their sanctified impulses of love. They assume so-and-so is just too busy to receive an invitation. Or they hear about a family going through a stressful time and feel an impulse to prepare a surprise meal, but the stirring is quenched by shyness. They negate the "I want to help them" impulse with the thought, "But I'm not as close to them as other people." Instead of fleshing out their love, they just let it go. We really do need each other, but the "it's-harder-to-give" folks don't believe that includes them.

The "it's-harder-to-receive" types often burn bright the candle of mission and care for others, but it's nearly impossible for them to say "I need you." It's the Peter

Coming to the table is not just thinking, "I need food." It is also living, "I need you."

protest: "No, you will never wash my feet." (John 13:8) Sometimes they build an impenetrable relational wall with their inability to say no to tasks. Sometimes these folks have never tasted the wholesome grace of acceptance in the homes from which they came, so they pour themselves in the care of others, ignoring that they themselves have needs.

Proverbs 3:27 counsels, "Do not withhold any good thing when it is in your power to do it." Meals don't share themselves; people do. As members of the body of Christ, we fit together, mature together, by being givers *and* receivers. Pause to appreciate that God made you to be a whole giver-receiver. This is who you are. Now go take who you are into your faith community with freedom. Your table is a treasure given by God to grow love in your church. Be a giver. Be a receiver. Watch what God will do.

I'll never forget the invitation to have dinner with a newly married Ethiopian couple. We ate Ethiopian style—no plates or flatware. Platters of colorful cuisine steamed and sizzled. After the blessing, we tore off the large, spongy, pancake-like bread called *injera* and stuffed it with an array of choices—sautéed lamb and beef, hot sauce, cabbage, onions, lentils, and spinach. Getting the hand-packed delicacy to our mouths required letting go of tidiness. I overpacked my portion, but my clumsiness was soothed by the obvious pleasure of our hosts. What a messy joy. We needed this meal for more reasons than being hungry. We needed table life with our new friends. We felt their love. We saw their delight. We tasted their culture. The world became a more intimate place. We humbly received; the immigrants gave.

Your local church uniquely expresses the kingdom of God; you contribute to its glory. The word *hospitality* literally means "to love a stranger." The Food Network stars and trendy cooking magazines don't ask this of us, but Jesus does. Loving the stranger calls us beyond the times and places of our familiar site of worship. It takes us out of our comfort zones. Your faith community is where taking the risk of loving the stranger begins. (If we don't do it there, will we do it elsewhere?) Do the hard thing—step out of your comfort zone. A personal greeting and an open door are not little things; they are the Christ-life.

Bulky key chains annoy my husband—the fewer the keys, the better. But hospitality is the one key worth carrying because it unlocks many doors to love. It's so remarkably simple. We love *simply* by sharing a meal. Love isn't as complicated as we sometimes make it. Reaching out to a person we don't know is love. Of course, we're also free to enjoy sipping coffee with a best friend—Jesus made the coffee bean for just such an occasion! But just remember, you've been in the crowd when the stranger was you.

Begin by asking God to open your eyes, and listen to God's holy nudge. You may notice someone you've seen many times, but the thought to share a meal has never crossed your mind. Do it! If the timing isn't right for sharing your leftover meat loaf or takeout pad thai, then just take a breath and begin by introducing yourself to the "stranger" in the crowd. "Hi, my name's Joanne. I'm glad to meet you." Greeting opens a gateway to table life. It expresses kindness and prepares a path to open your front door. Children naturally live this way. A child makes a new friend in class and then runs to Mom, pleading, "Can Stephanie come to our house today?" Lord, teach us to be like children.

I know from experience that awkward moments make us squirm. Have you ever greeted someone as if she's a newcomer, only to learn she's been around for years? I have. Roger and I had a good laugh at our table when our guest Kimberly said that every time Roger saw her, he called her by the wrong name. Have you ever looked away from someone walking toward you, because you couldn't remember his name? Be interdependent. Go up to him and say, "I need your help. I know I've met you before, but would you remind me of your name?" Our names do matter. Begin by learning a few. Most of us don't have the knack for remembering names, so jot down a new name or say it a couple times in your first conversation. Repetition helps.

And we must not forget there are those among the people of God who do not know God. I heard a story of a woman who decided to see if she could find God at church. Every Sunday after the service, the pastor opened a time for questions and conversation. Several weeks passed, and finally the woman said, "I just have one question. What's the *T* hanging on the wall?" The cross! She didn't understand the cross. Now imagine if you sat next to her. Taking a moment to notice the person sitting next to you might be the first step to introducing someone to Jesus. How would you give her a taste of the glad welcome of God? Imagine how much she could learn about God's love by sharing a meal with his followers.

Interdependence is good for everyone, regardless of marital status. Singles invite couples and couples invite singles. If you are married, learning to do hospitality together adds blessing to your marriage. Bill and Judy tell their story.

As newlyweds almost forty years ago, we lived in a small duplex just two blocks from our church. We were busy. I worked as an RN on the evening hospital shift, and my husband was a second-year

Oh Dear!

We participated in "Triad Dinners," matching up three families who would take turns hosting a meal. When our turn came, I excitedly prepared my classic, can't-miss baked beef stew recipe. I turned on the oven just as we left for church. All morning while we were out, I imagined the aroma in the house and mentally rehearsed serving the stew with pleasure. But upon returning home, we were shocked to discover no hint of aroma. In fact, the oven was stone cold! When I asked my family, it was our sixteen-year old daughter who said, "When I walked past the oven to leave for church, I saw that you had left it on. So I turned it off."

I panicked. We had promised them beef stew, so I dispatched my husband to fly to the quickest quick-mart to pick up three large cans of Dinty Moore Beef Stew. He returned before the other families arrived, and we were able to heat it up in a saucepan undetected. Not only was our gathering full of sharing and laughter, their sixteen-year-old son asked me for the recipe before he left!

—Terri and Jackie

medical student. But we loved opening our apartment to groups of young adults. Often there were forty to fifty pairs of flip-flops piled at our front door. We had a few pieces of hand-me-down furniture, and one of our two bedrooms was filled with wedding gifts left in their original boxes for an anticipated move the following year. The menu was never fancy, but it's amazing how many young adults you can attract with a big pot of chili, hot dogs, and rice. In this tiny and not-so-perfect venue, we learned to share what little we had. We built some of our closest lifelong friendships and shared many unforgettable meals with a wide range of friends and family.

Men, if you're at all like my husband, you have a favorite chair or well-sculpted spot on the end of the couch. For many men, home means, "I need a haven. Let me take off the harness of responsibilities and rest." Rest is a good thing, but many men are content to let their wives "do the hospitality thing." Whether your wife works outside the home or is a full-time homemaker, your home will impact others if you practice hospitality *together*—in spirit as well as in tasks. It's living the Christ-life through your marriage. And your wife will love it. Couples can individually work through the details of what needs to be done. I make the soup and bread; Roger scoops the sherbet, gets the wood burning in the fireplace, and helps serve the meal. Together, we anticipate the guests, and when they leave, we clear the dishes and reminisce about the stories and people who came to our table. And before we put our heads on our pillows, we pray for each one. In the naturalness of having shared our home together, we practice the presence of Christ together.

Couples who pursue hospitality together grow closer in their marriage as they work out the details with understanding. My friend Laura admits this can be a challenge. She and her husband, John, like having friends over, but Laura often feels the details get dumped on her watch. Unfulfilled expectations quench her joy and break communication with John. She realizes she needs to verbalize a few clearly stated requests to John, say no to her own perfectionism, and create ways to make the process fun together.

Roger and I do this life together because during college and our newly married years, other couples mentored us with this lifestyle: Jerry and Allegra, Wes and Judy, Jan and Chick, Sherwin and Pat, Bill and Judi, Joe and Cathy, Betsy and Brownie. I dream and pray for living churches to be ignited by this life of love. Before we were married, Roger experienced true hospitality from Betsy and Brownie, who were known as the B's:

An uncommon welcome happened during my sophomore year of college. After a cross-country race, I broke into a high fever. College health care being practically nonexistent, I staggered to a doctor and discovered I had mononucleosis. My roommate had zero nurturing capacity, so I called Betsy Brown. I knew Betsy, a cook extraordinaire, and her husband, Brownie, a meat cutter, from our church. Periodically, they invited students home for dinner after church. We fed on meat never seen in the college dining commons: T-bones, sirloin tip, prime rib. Their succulent and lavish table offered a feast of regal dimensions.

This time, I called the Browns because I knew their hearts. Hospitality builds trust in relationships, and I needed them. Though they had no way of knowing my virulent and contagious condition, they instantly welcomed me. I slept, drank tea, sipped soup, sweated through sheets, and deliriously lost track of an entire week under their care. Together they created a safe, warm, caring home away from the dorm for a hapless convalescent. When the hospitality hall of fame is revealed in heaven, Betsy and Brownie will be in it!

Jesus calls us to embrace interdependence in all seasons of life. Each season brings new challenges. But one season has a unique opportunity to unleash love in the living church—the empty nest. I've never liked that phrase; it sounds so vacant. I prefer calling it the "rearranged nest." Although our daughters have gone on to raise families of their own, we haven't downsized yet. When that day comes, my dining room table moves with us.

Many empty-nesters feel the pinch in a new role as the "sandwich generation." Caring for aged parents and making room for boomerang adult children is an exhausting stretch that often limits hospitality to the extended family. This sacrificial devotion honors God. But after those needs pass—and we've taken time to rest and recover—the opportunity for hospitality knocks at our doors. The living church needs dreamers whose dreams about the retirement years include a passionate commitment to table life.

Our Western culture tends to isolate the different generations, whereas a biblical worldview calls for a common life where generations meet at the table to share wisdom, ask questions, shed a few tears, explore possibilities, and celebrate faith...while sipping smoothies poured from the kitchen blender. Sometimes the coffee shop works just fine for young and old alike, but your home shares more of you. We need to learn to linger like the Lord. It's for all of us.

Taste and See

It's not uncommon for recipes to get retitled according to the enthusiastic preferences of our children. I have a well-worn, splattered recipe card titled, "Shelly's Noodles." I'm pretty sure most any child would love to eat this for dinner. And here's a love-idea for those of you past the baby-and-toddler stage of parenting:

Recall a recipe your kids liked, then surprise a young, exhausted mother with a home delivery or an invitation to your table for this favorite kid meal.

Shelly's Noodles

1½ cups small-shell noodles
1 pound ground beef or turkey
1 small onion, minced
One 8-ounce can tomato sauce
½ cup milk or water
⅛ teaspoon Worcestershire sauce
½ cup grated cheese
Salt and pepper to taste
Dash celery salt

Cook noodles, drain, and rinse. Brown hamburger, drain fat. Mix in remaining ingredients. Bake 45 minutes at 325°F.

(Note: One way to sneak healthy veggies into this meal is adding some chopped kale or spinach just after you have browned the meat.)

Daily Bread

"And since we are all one body in Christ, we belong to each other and each of us needs all the others." (Romans 12:5b *NLT*)

Prayer

Make me whole, Lord. So often I feel fractured, imbalanced, out of breath. Help me live interdependently. Forgive me when I give without a humble willingness to receive. Thank you for making me a part of your family. In Jesus' name, amen.

Altar Call

Savoring the presence of Jesus at your table creates a heart of humility.

CHAPTER 4

Surprise!

Jesus the guest brings an unexpected gift to the table.

The Jesus Table

It's Sunday afternoon. Two friends, bonded by their common affection for Jesus, walk seven miles home with their backs to Jerusalem as the city's mighty limestone ramparts diminish like vanishing hope. Perplexed, their minds strain to make sense of a rumor they just heard. Supposedly, the body of their crucified teacher was not in the grave, and angels had announced to some women that Jesus was alive.

Their private conversation spins like a spider's web until the weight of their confusion collapses into sadness. Along the way, a curious stranger catches up with them and asks, "What are you so concerned about?" (Luke 24:17, *NLT*) Shocked by his ignorance, his question stops them like a stone wall. They figure everybody knows about Friday's crucifixion. They tell the stranger Jesus' story, not realizing they stand in the presence of Jesus himself.

Their bewilderment intensifies. The stranger is with them, but they feel alone, absorbed in thought. They know Jesus was a prophet and rabbi. His teaching surpassed religious eloquence; it was like music that captured their yearning hearts with a melody of eternity. For some time, they thought he might be the Messiah. But as reason collides with the cross, grief storms their faith.

"BY THIS TIME THEY WERE NEARING EMMAUS AND THE END OF THEIR JOURNEY. JESUS WOULD HAVE GONE ON, BUT THEY BEGGED HIM TO STAY THE NIGHT WITH THEM, SINCE IT WAS GETTING LATE. SO HE WENT HOME WITH THEM. AS THEY SAT DOWN TO EAT, HE TOOK A SMALL LOAF OF BREAD, ASKED GOD'S BLESSING ON IT, THEN GAVE IT TO THEM. SUDDENLY, THEIR EYES WERE OPENED AND THEY RECOGNIZED HIM."

(Luke 24:28–31)

In this confusing moment on the Emmaus road, Jesus says, "You are such foolish people. You find it so hard to believe all that the prophets wrote in the Scriptures." (Luke 24:25, *NLT*) What peculiar words at a time of sorrow, the men think! Jesus tells his friends they are dull; they don't yet comprehend he is the Lamb of God who takes away sin. They're sad, but Jesus wants them to dance. They're informed, but they're not yet changed. Something is missing. It sounds harsh to tell friends they are dull, but it's not a hammer of shame. Christ wants to jar their minds to see the truth: The Messiah comes to be a suffering savior.

Jesus cues the friends to walk farther. He knows they need time to absorb his rebuke, and soon it will be dark. His kind pace soothes them, and his voice offers the strength of a brother's love. A mysterious wonder sneaks into the evening air, provoking the friends with a nagging question—who is this man who teaches us? Only resurrection power restrains Jesus from grabbing their cloaks and shouting, "I am the Lord!" *He's waiting for just the right time to reveal himself.*

The edge of night falls as they come to a fork in the road that turns toward Emmaus. Jesus pauses, then steps away, as if to leave them. But the two friends want more of this pedestrian stranger, so they urge him to come to their house for dinner. He gladly follows them home, washes, and waits while they set the table. Then he does the unexpected: He reaches for the bread, gives thanks, and breaks it. Suddenly, the confused mourners recognize Jesus. But instantly, he disappears. The table of three becomes a table of two.

The two friends sit at the table, face to face, stunned by the realization that they had just been with Jesus himself. Can't you picture their riveted stare, their arms spread on the table as if they were holding heavy sacks of jewels, ready to fling joy into the silent night? Their Emmaus road lesson plunges from head to heart. The stone of unbelief rolls away. And it happens at the table!

Don't race past this dinner. Remember, the epiphany came when Jesus took the bread, broke the bread, blessed the bread, and gave the bread. Breaking bread is a treasure to God. Scripture leaves many details untold, but my hunch is that these friends had experienced the intimacy of the table with Jesus several times before. Our hands are like our faces; they identify us. If they had eaten with Jesus often, not only did they recognize *how* he broke bread, but they also knew the size of his hands, the ridges of his fingernails, and the map of veins on the back of his hands. Reaching for a loaf of bread required Jesus to stretch and then turn his palms vertically as he took the loaf by its rounded edges. This motion would show the wounds in his wrist.

Transformed and unhindered by night's darkness, Cleopas and his friend run to another home-gathering back in Jerusalem to tell the truth about the risen Lord to the eleven disciples, who are huddling in their sadness. "While they were still talking about this, Jesus himself stood among them and said to them, 'peace be with you.'" (John 24:36) Then Jesus transforms the shock of their fright into joy by asking for some fish to eat. "He took it and ate it in their presence." (Luke 14:43) If there were ever a day for God to surprise frail humanity, it was this day as they watched the risen Lord eat fish.

✦ ✦ ✦ ✦ ✦ ✦ ✦ ✦ ✦ ✦ ✦ ✦ ✦

God opens our eyes to see him. He initiates, prepares, moves, works, and gives liberally. And he's jealous for us to recognize his presence in common places. The God who reveals himself in the expanse of the heavens also loves to reveal himself in the intimacy of the table. God doesn't just bless the bread; he yearns to bless us.

Breaking bread is a treasure to God.

Jesus has a consistent pattern both before and after his Resurrection. The surprise gift he always brings to the table is a revelation of himself—forgiveness, hope, intimacy, guidance, and blessing. His actual presence. From the home of Zacchaeus, the very short man; to the wedding dinner at Cana; to a meal with pouting Pharisees; to the Acts 1 dinner huddle before his Ascension, Christ always came to the table with a gift, a revelation of himself.

Finding Your Table

Jesus didn't camp outside the empty tomb or preach a sermon at his execution site to testify to his resurrection power. He went to eat fish with friends in the personal space of home. Now view this event from the perspective of Jesus preparing the disciples for his Ascension: He promised to send them his Holy Spirit. Later, the apostle Paul wrote, "The grace of the Lord Jesus Christ, the love of God, and the communion of the Holy Spirit be with all of you." (2 Corinthians 13:13) This blessing aptly describes table life. The triune God dines with his children; not in the flesh, but through the Spirit.

We know this, but do we watch for it? Do we believe Jesus reveals himself at our tables? What is our orientation as we invite, prepare, and receive others, or as we go to another's home? What's our primary focus? Are we prayerfully expectant that Christ's presence will be enjoyed, or are we so obsessed with details, that this faith perspective is neglected? As children, our daughters frequently asked, "What's for dinner?" and "Who's coming for dinner?" Do you hear the faith in those questions? They're great questions to ask. The place where your table and the gospel story meet is faith—*believing* that Christ is coming for dinner and the real meal is fellowship with him.

Are we prayerfully expectant that Christ's presence will be enjoyed, or are we so obsessed with details that the faith perspective is neglected?

We need to cultivate an attitude of faith. Unbelief makes hospitality less than it's designed to be, like omitting the apples from an apple pie. Hospitality without faith saps our energy. The apostle Paul wrote, "The only thing that counts is faith expressing itself in love." (Galatians 5:6) Whether we're inviting our best friends or international students we meet in the library checkout line, the sure way to love is to believe Jesus will be with us when we share a meal.

Weeds of unbelief can sprout in our hearts like dandelions on a warm spring day. A few years ago, a herniated disc sidelined me to the waiting room of excruciating pain, surgery, and slow recovery. Many brought Christ's table to me with lovingly prepared meals; I learned to be a receiver. But with the passing months, our own table collected dust, and I wondered if we'd ever open our front door again. That day finally and mercifully arrived, but a weed of unbelief sprang up just hours before the guests arrived.

While fixing the soup and bread, a random thought that had nothing to do with dinner suddenly popped into my mind: *Where are our tickets?* After a frantic search, I fumed and fussed that the airline tickets for our Christmas in Houston, which had been last seen in my desk, were now lost, apparently tossed out with paid bills in the waste basket and taken to the dump by our reliable trash service. My carelessness momentarily hijacked my focus of faith. But I chose to do the next right thing: I set aside the distraction and remembered what mattered for the moment. I had almost let a human foible smother my faith. But faith won. Christ came. I experienced his kindness by tasting the miracle of being raised to eat a meal again with the family of God.

Lifestyle Check: Do I anticipate and look for the unseen real presence of Jesus at my table? Do I take time to reflect back on Christ's presence at the meal after the guests have gone home?

Heart Check: Do I believe Jesus will reveal himself at my table?

Setting Your Table

Coming to the table is not just about tasting food; it's also about experiencing the unseen, real presence of Christ. "Oh taste and see that the Lord is good." (Psalms 34:8) It is eating with faith. Faith increases the pleasure of every meal. I've discovered the best way to eat with faith is to prepare with faith. Whether you prepare a meal of prime rib or ham and eggs, everything your hands touch can be a gift that opens your heart to believe God will reveal himself at your table. Even that milky juice dripping out of a sliced onion can prepare your heart with faith (along with tears).

As I lay the soup spoons on the table, I talk to Jesus. I thank him that he has known about this little gathering around my scratched mahogany table since before his dinner in Emmaus. Sometimes I need to tell him I'm tired or a bit grumpy, but by faith, I set the table. When I mince the garlic for the Mexican chicken soup and wonder if I've picked a too-spicy recipe, I thank God for his goodness in creating the gastronomical ingredients. As I pour water into the glasses, I ask Jesus to fill us with his love through his Spirit. Sometimes I go back in my imagination to one of the tables he ate at in Jerusalem or Capernaum.

These conversations with God prime my heart with faith. In this simple exercise, faith frames the evening. Maybe I forget to put the butter on the table, but my heart is in the right place. By the time we sit at the table, I have an expectancy that rests in God's good purposes. I may not know what those are, but I trust him to be actively working.

Christian hospitality is work infused with the promise of Christ's presence. The beauty of the table is that it creates time and space to *be attentive* to what Christ gives us. Jesus said, "Look! Here I stand at the door and knock. If you hear me calling and open the door, I will come in, and we will share a meal as friends." (Revelations 3:20) Notice the sequence of Christ's words: "look" (be attentive); "here I stand" (I'm here); "if you hear me calling" (show me your faith); "I will come" (this is my promise); and "we will share a meal as friends" (let's experience intimate joy while we eat a meal together).

My husband and I had the privilege of sitting around our table with a couple married forty-six years, a newlywed couple both previously divorced, a Chinese couple from Singapore, and a couple with young children. It was a diverse group, from the chiseled macho to the balding bold. While eating, we told our little stories—our work, hobbies, and the places we had lived. Such conversation always stimulates more questions. Halfway through the evening, it was obvious every couple was going through a significant transition. We didn't plan this; God did. Two of the couples I had never met before. But Christ had a serving of grace for each of us.

On this night, it was Dick's ability to talk freely about his relationship with Christ in the midst of difficulty that drew us to the riches of the meal. Everyone has struggles, but not everyone feels comfortable verbally expressing how faith in Jesus carries him or her through the hard times. But when just one person opens his heart, it's a gift to everyone. You can feel it. We all need joy; we want to believe there's more joy for us. Although I can't remember the exact details of what Dick shared, I remember the experience of love and joy fostered by his vulnerability and vibrant relationship to Christ. We leaned into the counsel of this wise, humble pilgrim. We sat around the table as brothers and sisters, but it was Dick's story that uniquely served a priestly role that Thursday night. It seemed just right that he and his wife happened to be sitting at the end of the table. We ate with joy. The food was fine, but Christ was the feast. It felt as if no one wanted to leave the table. Table life trumped the traffic of suburban life.

God's surprises are for your home, too. It's possible. It's nearer than you imagine. Christ is knocking. Honestly, just hours before that dinner, I was feeling blue—no, gray, like the January sky. I couldn't put my finger on the reason. It was just one of those low-grade, blah afternoons. It was definitely an "I'm doing this by faith" dinner preparation. But then my table became an altar where God took my modest act of faith to draw my heart close to his.

I hope it doesn't sound like dinner is a church service. It's simply a shared meal, done by faith. But yes, preparing your table is an act of worship. Hospitality isn't just what some people do; it's what believers do. "They broke bread in their homes and ate together with glad and sincere hearts, praising God and enjoying the favor of all people." (Acts 2:46) Believers don't just eat to live; they also live to eat—with each other.

There are as many ways to use the table as there are people. Table life is more about faith and function (why you do it) than it is about form (how you do it). Method is fluid and shaped by the occasion, plans, and your unique personality. My friend Cheri loves God, and her eyes glint with mischief. What a combination. I'll never forget her "Dump Stew" night, where she dumped the meal on butcher paper spread across the table.

Opening our homes is obedience to God. As parents, we understand the importance of obedience, but it's a learning curve for our children. In Romans 12:13, the apostle Paul wrote to God's children in Rome, "Practice hospitality." This word *practice* literally means "pursue." This is a command given in the context of urging believers to present themselves to God as living sacrifices. To pursue hospitality out of obedience is to "plan for it, prepare for it, pray about it, and seek opportunities to do it."[1] We're motivated to push through anxieties and fears by believing Christ's words, "If you obey my commands you will remain in my love, just as I have obeyed my Father's commands and remain in his love. I have told you this so that my joy may be in you and that your joy may be complete." (John 15:10–11) Pursuing hospitality increases our experience of God's love and joy.

Here are a few practical ideas that have helped our household reach beyond our comfort zone. Imagine inviting several guests who have never met. It doesn't have to feel like the nervous first steps in a dance class. After our guests arrive and peel off layers of Minnesota insulation, we give them name tags. Some people have an aversion for name tags in a crowd; they prefer anonymity. But with a small group, it gives security and instantly provides something to do—peel the backside paper off the tag.

Then we give our guests a card to write their names, work, hobbies, and one thing about themselves we would not normally learn in passing conversation. Some scratch their heads at the last question, convinced they have nothing interesting to share, while others write

Oh Dear!

It was a Saturday afternoon, and I felt well-prepared for the Christmas party that night. So it didn't bother me at all when two international students dropped by for a visit. We were having a grand time catching up, when I noticed the clock. It was time to get the potatoes in the oven. I reached into the refrigerator to pull out what I thought was the pan of scalloped potatoes covered in foil, but it was actually my layered Jell-O salad.

As guest arrived dressed in beautiful Christmas cheer, I welcomed them with a hug. When I reached in the oven to pull the taters, out came the red Jell-O with cream cheese and fruit bubbling like a mud pot at Yellowstone! Of course, I tried to be cool and not completely freak out, so I stalled the meal as I tried to nuke the scalloped potatoes in the microwave and throw together a fruit salad with cans from my pantry. As a Southern cook, the goal is not to let them see you sweat, right? So I was absolutely "radiant" when we sat down to pray!

—Pat

The beauty of the table is that it can be a safe place for sharing the heart.

of wild conquests. But once the storytelling begins, the sharing creates a table adventure together. Part of the fun is having each person "introduce" the person next to him by reading his card. It feels like you're holding a chapter of someone's autobiography. Oftentimes the autobiographies grow as others at the table ask more questions. Respectful curiosity celebrates the person. Everyone's story matters.

Another idea is to place on your table something that symbolizes an experience or life lesson of faith and describe it to your guests. The beauty of the table is that it can be a safe place for sharing the heart. As we experienced that night with Dick, once someone shares a bit of his heart, something shifts. We can't force it, but we can pray for it and create some prompters. That's what a symbol on the table can do. Because every believer has the Spirit of God living within, we have a divine capacity to "Speak to one another with psalms, hymns and spiritual songs" (Ephesians 5:19). In other words, we are made to talk about the Lord's working in our lives. You'll be amazed to discover how conversation will flow from kids, jobs, food, and vacations to a celebration of our faithful God. These discussions are nutrients for the soul of God's children.

Your symbol on the table can be anything; just pick something whose faith meaning you'll be able to clearly explain. Then give your guests an opportunity to share how it relates to their faith story. (There will probably be a pause, but don't let the silence bother you. Trust God to animate the sharing.) The symbol might be a rock, representing God's strength that has carried you from fear to love. Or a shoestring taken from a well-worn running shoe, symbolizing a lesson learned on perseverance. What's most important is that you connect your story with the symbol.

At our house, we often use three symbols: bread, salt, and a cup for wine. To begin the meal, I explain it was common in the Jewish home for these three symbols to be placed on the table. The bread represents provision, the salt represents sacrifice (salt was always thrown on the altar), and the cup of wine represents joy. Every Old Testament Jew had these symbols "talking to them" as they ate dinner. This practice was continued in the early church. After that very brief history lesson, we slurp soup and smear butter on bread as we tell our little stories. Then later, while cleaning our palates with sherbet, we come back to the symbols and spend a few minutes sharing personal stories of God's provision, redemption, and joy.

A beautiful outcome of this practice is that it naturally leads to praying together at the close of the evening. In just two hours, we've heard about hobbies and hardships, but we've also remembered the loving God to whom we belong. Praying at the close of a meal is actually a fulfillment of the command in Deuteronomy 6:11b: "When you eat and are satisfied, be careful that you do not forget the Lord." Our prayer time is brief, sweet, and specific. We pray for any needs that have been expressed, but the greater glory is how God uses the prayers to reveal the love received from him just because we took time to eat a meal together.

The author of Hebrews wrote, "Keep loving each other as brothers. Do not forget to entertain strangers, for by so doing some people have entertained angels without knowing it." (Hebrews 13:2) Several months ago, we were wakened by a phone call at 10:40 P.M. On the other end was a woman by the name of Rachel, who was stranded at the Minneapolis airport. A fierce windstorm had shut down everything, and all the hotels were booked. She had just arrived from England, en route to see her first grandchild in Wisconsin. Through connections I still don't understand, she got our name and number. She had a lovely British accent and sounded cordial, so we asked, "How can we identify you?" She replied, "I'm wearing a bright yellow jacket." As I did a quick once-over of the guest room, Roger picked her up at the airport.

After a good night's sleep, we had breakfast together. As we sat at the table eating steel-cut oats, the question crossed my mind, "I wonder if Rachel is one of those 'angels unaware'?" Her story of God healing her body at a near-death experience brought a timely word of encouragement as I thought about the physical needs of our granddaughter. So I asked Rachel to pray for her. Her radiant faith strengthened my heart, and when I took her back to the airport to continue onto her destination, my question lingered—"Is she an angel?"

Love, mystery, and meals are calling. Cleopas unknowingly ate not with an angel, but with the Lord. Let the Lord's surprises live in your home, too.

✦ ✦ ✦ ✦ ✦ ✦ ✦ ✦ ✦ ✦ ✦ ✦ ✦

It was a peculiar night. Earlier in the day, Max called to say he would be driving his semitrailer through the Twin Cities and asked if he could stop by. We hadn't seen our Denver friend Max for years, but it was a Monday—our only day off together. Activities had taken us in separate directions all week, so we were looking forward to a dinner evening for two. With a twinge of reluctance, we wondered if a change of plans would be a dutiful disruption or a surrender to surprise.

Since Max's rig was too large for the neighborhood, Roger arranged to meet him at the church parking lot, then they returned to our home for freshly fried fish and leftover spareribs. Max ate as if he hadn't been out of his truck in days. Our shy guest wooed me into his kind, rumpled presence as he talked about our Denver days as if he were reading entries from a diary. I couldn't believe the minutiae he remembered that had long faded from my memory. He wasn't talking a blue streak.

His conversation was more like a needle and thread rising from a hand-stitched hem. My sadness came when his eyes dropped low, like a needle pushed back down into silence. In that passing moment, he felt like a fidgety boy who wasn't sure what to say next. I wanted to reach across the table to lift his face and coax his shame away.

After eating pecan brittle ice cream, Max mentioned he brought film footage of his Army days in Vietnam. He had been a transport driver during the war. We popped the video into our player. The scratchy, silent images on our television carved an eerie knothole into the past as we listened to his live commentary from our green couch. It was fascinating yet dismal. I wondered how many times he had watched this by himself.

As Max prepared to leave, he shyly gave me a gift wrapped in obvious haste—a small maple-leaf-shaped bottle gleaming with golden Canadian maple syrup. We prayed for traveling mercies and the comfort of God's love for the thousands of miles stretching ahead. I asked how soon he would be seeing his wife and two children. He didn't know.

Max was rolling down the highway hundreds of miles away from our front door the following morning when I thought back to our time together. I had almost missed the wonder of this night. Hospitality fueled by a living faith *expects* God to be present and active at every shared meal. I was glad we had opened our front door to Max, but God wanted to take me beyond mere recognition of his hand at work to a change in my heart. He deepened my faith as I took time to look at and listen to the undeniable evidence that he had prepared this table for eternal purposes.

Thirty minutes before Max's arrival, a die-hard fisherman from church who had promised us a fish fry just happened to knock on our door with a plate mounded with fish, green beans, and cornbread. The spareribs were leftovers from a barbeque we attended the day before. Our missionary friends had contributed the ice cream at a dinner together the previous Friday. As I thought about God's potluck, my heart went from laughter to tears to worship. After setting our reluctance aside, setting our table for one more person seemed as ordinary as the flimsy, generic napkins tucked under the forks. But like Moses standing before a bush in the wilderness, we discovered the table was a divine appointment aflame with God's love. And all I had to do was rearrange my plans.

We never know everything God is doing at the table. Often his work is hidden. Sometimes it's to relieve our stress with laughter. Sometimes it brings a deep healing for the soul. Few of us live in the cab of a truck, many of us live in the fast lane of life, but all of us need a place at the table.

I have a hunch that wherever Max is traveling today, he savors the memory of that Monday night. That's where my heart dwells. Thank you, Lord, for hosting the table and changing my heart. Our tables are designed by God to dynamically acknowledge Christ's presence. Cultivate a habit of remembering the ways God has shown up at your table. Talk about it, think about it. Let yesterday's gifts create anticipation for tomorrow's surprises.

Taste and See

Just as the experience of Christ's presence makes all the difference in our ordinary days, the smallest hint of spice often transforms an ordinary recipe into a gourmet delight. When my friend Laurie gave me this recipe, she said, "The secret is the anise." This is one of our favorite soups—so comforting!

Did You Know?

"In early English usage…to converse was to foster community, to commune with, to dwell in a place with others. Conversation was understood to be a life-sustaining practice, a blessing, and a craft to be cultivated for the common good." [2] *Consider the differences between conversation around a shared meal and conversations via texting, e-mail, and Facebook.*

Tomato Chicken Soup

2 tablespoons butter or oil
1 large onion
4 ounces cream cheese
30 ounces tomato sauce
4 cups milk
2 cloves garlic, minced
2 cubes chicken bouillon
1 chicken, deboned
3 tomatoes, chopped
1 tablespoon hot sauce
1 teaspoon anise
2 zucchini, chopped

Melt butter or oil and sauté onion. Stir in cream cheese. Add tomato sauce, milk, garlic, bouillon, chicken, tomatoes, hot sauce, and anise. Add zucchini 30 minutes before serving. (Note: Instead of using bouillon, which is high in salt, I make a broth by simmering the chicken bones several hours. I then decrease the milk by 1 cup and add as much broth as I need to feed the crowd.)

Daily Bread

"Oh taste and see that the Lord is good." (Psalms 34:8)

Prayer

Father, I often leave out faith when I come to the table. Forgive me. Fill me with faith. May every meal I share be a taste of your goodness, a recognition of your real presence. In Jesus' name, amen.

Altar Call

Savoring the presence of Jesus at your table creates a heart of faith.

CHAPTER 5

Don't Fuss

Jesus the host brings freedom to the table.

The Jesus Table

Jesus never owned a home. He didn't lease an apartment or furnish a condo. He never got to say, "Come on over to my house." He was completely dependent on the hospitality of others, yet it did not define his role at the table. When Christ entered a home, the table turned to a whole new order. Let's look at an example of this.

Jesus has just explained the true meaning of being a neighbor by telling the story of the Good Samaritan. Now he walks to Bethany, a village two miles southeast of Jerusalem. Dinner brings him and several disciples to the home of Martha, who gives Jesus an enthusiastic welcome. She—along with her younger sister, Mary, and their brother, Lazarus—has been anticipating his arrival for hours. Jesus feels completely at home with his generous friends. He's hungry, but since dinner isn't quite ready, Martha is relieved Jesus waits with his typical kind demeanor. Martha scoots to the kitchen while Mary sits and listens devotedly to Jesus.

As minutes pass, the heat in the kitchen rises, but it's not because of the oven. Martha is miffed. All the guests notice her agitation—the clanging pots and body language tell all. Even the children notice. Martha goes to Jesus and complains, "Lord, don't you care that my sister has left me to do the work by myself? Tell her to

> "AS JESUS AND HIS DISCIPLES WERE ON THEIR WAY, HE CAME TO A VILLAGE WHERE A WOMAN NAMED MARTHA OPENED HER HOME TO HIM. SHE HAD A SISTER CALLED MARY, WHO SAT AT THE LORD'S FEET LISTENING TO WHAT HE SAID. BUT MARTHA WAS DISTRACTED BY ALL THE PREPARATIONS THAT HAD TO BE MADE."
>
> (Luke 10:38–40)

help me!" (Luke 10:40) Mary winces and sheepishly defers to Jesus with a bewildered look. She hopes he will soothe this awkward drama in the living room. Jesus says to Martha, "Martha, Martha, you are anxious and troubled about many things, but one thing is necessary. Mary has chosen the good portion, which will not be taken away from her." (Luke 10:41)

We don't know exactly what irritated Martha the most. Was it that she wanted Mary to peel carrots, or was it that she, too, wanted to listen to Jesus with unfettered devotion? Only God knows. Certainly, Mary made a habit of willingly helping her sister in the kitchen, and Martha genuinely loved to serve meals. Although it's reasonable for Martha to want some help, how she handled her expectation revealed the deeper issue—pride. She let comparison and performance take precedence over a glad surrender to the Lord's presence.

Jesus cut through the tense moment of this pre-meal meltdown with grace and truth. And amazing courage! What a delicate situation. Jesus cared so deeply for Martha, he responded to her complaint with bold love. When Jesus tenderly appealed to Martha by saying her name twice—"Martha, Martha"—we get a glimpse of the depth of his love and longing for her to be set free. In this conversation, Jesus invited Martha to take a new step of faith: *Don't look at your sister. Look at me!* Jesus wanted Martha to surrender her culinary competence to his divine presence.

This doesn't cancel out Jesus' gratitude for Martha's open home and signature meals—he still wanted and appreciated them! He wasn't devaluing the worth of Martha's service or scowling at the cook while making Mary the teacher's pet. Christ's goal was to love Martha into her full benefits as a daughter of the King. He wanted her to embrace a liberating truth: Jesus is the true host of every

God-centered table. She needed to set her heart free from the enslaving inclination to compete, compare, and perform—all forms of pride.

To appreciate the bold love of this narrative, we need to go to the beginning of the text in Luke 10:38. It begins with these words: "Jesus and his disciples were on their way...." Notice the author Luke uses Christ's common name, Jesus. Friends are going to friends' home. But through the rest of the story, Luke uses the name Lord. Christ is friend *and* Christ is Lord. Even Martha uses the name Lord: "She came to him and asked, 'Lord, don't you care that my sister has left me to do the work by myself?" (Luke 10:40)

Martha has no idea her complaint offends the Lord. Scripture doesn't tell what happens after the Lord's rebuke. Maybe Martha let the stew simmer without the carrots. If her heart hardened with pride, it would have been a tense meal. But I believe the meal was a healing balm for Martha. Christ honors women, and I doubt he let Martha hide in the kitchen. When it was time to eat, it's reasonable to assume Christ was asked to give the blessing. Imagine Martha's sulkiness wilting as Jesus expressed thanks to his Father for food and friends. Grace convinces me that Jesus enjoyed the food, infused the conversation with gratitude, and kindly looked for light in Martha's repentant eyes as she served him, the true host of her table.

If you think this imaginative final scene is off target, consider the "new" Martha we meet later in John 12. She's still a competent cook, but with a different spirit. This meal celebrated Lazarus being raised from the stinking tomb. No doubt Martha's menu was a knockout, five-star extravaganza; this party deserved more than cashew butter spread on celery sticks. "Martha served...then Mary took about a pint of pure nard, an expensive perfume; she poured it on Jesus' feet and wiped

"A meal of bread and water in contented peace is better than a banquet spiced with quarrels." Proverbs 17:1, The Message

his feet with her hair. And the house was filled with the fragrance of the perfume." (John 12:2–3)

Martha's liberation appears in between the lines of this narrative. It's a feast without fury. No "by-myself" tantrums. No sibling rivalry. No huffy, sanctified pride. Martha didn't fuss that the perfume competed with the sautéed lamb. Both sisters simply devoted their hearts to Jesus. The honored guest was the unrivaled host of two surrendered, faith-filled women. Demands, comparison, perfectionism, and performance died; the pursuit of their hospitality was pure heart.

Finding Your Table

We're all tempted to fuss about house and meals. And it's disappointing to realize how the quick trigger of pride keeps us from opening our front doors. Sharing crème brûlée at trendy cafés doesn't feel as difficult as sharing chips and dip in our homes. Isn't that crazy? We say, "There's no place like home" because it feels comfy and safe; that is, until our thoughts wander to the rickety folding chairs or the worn-out carpet. The time crunch of the twenty-first century isn't the only thing that keeps us from opening our homes. The age-old afflictions of perfectionism and comparison handcuff our hearts from pursuing hospitality.

Table life is a call to both men and women, but women tend to be more disposed to pride—and along with it, perfectionism and comparison—in the context of the personal space of home. You can take women out of the home, but you can't take home out of the heart of women. We love home. That's why we buy buckets of paint and plant red geraniums in clay pots. We have a nurturing instinct that longs to create beauty where we live. Beauty nurtures us. These longings are like spring waters in our souls; they're good and God given, but they're easily polluted.

To find our tables, we need to identify the pollutants that threaten the authentic beauty of hospitality. Hospitality is people centered. It loves God by loving people. When performance and possessions define who we are and what we do, we're likely to exchange beauty for a lie.

Respond to the following statements with "never," "sometimes," or "often."

1. I compare the size of my home to others' and feel it's inadequate.

2. I feel it's more important that everything be "just right" instead of "just enough."

3. I feel like a failure when I think about how other people entertain.

4. I feel I'll never be able to fulfill the standards my mother set.

Comparison, a form of pride, is the vulnerability of every woman's heart. I've heard it said, "Comparison is to a woman's heart what lust is to a man's heart." It's our downfall. The lie that binds and never satisfies is that one that whispers, "Hospitality is about *me* and my stuff." God is grieved by the sinful habit of comparison that takes our eyes off his son Christ and keeps our tables to ourselves. Author Sharon Hersh writes, "Comparisons involve quantifying and measuring one thing against another, an activity that has to do with the 'material.' The danger of comparison is that it locks us into the material. Comparisons seduce us into wanting more and more and never enjoying what we already have.... Not only do comparisons keep us occupied with superficial concerns, but they diminish our capacity for relationships."[1]

When are you prone to inhale the toxin of comparison? It's like carbon monoxide; you can't see it or smell it, but it destroys life. Comparison is idolatry because its focus is self, and it causes the joy of love to evaporate, like boiling water over the hot flame of pride. Christ invites us to a more excellent way.

Comparison, a form of pride, is the vulnerability of every woman's heart.

75

Lifestyle Check: I'm most likely to fuss and compare when...

Heart Check: I know I'm envying other people's homes and abilities when...

Oh Dear!

Before my wedding, my parents invited my future in-laws for dinner. Normally I wouldn't be nervous because my parents often hosted guests for supper. Mom's casual style offered a "take us as we are" comfortable hospitality. But I wondered if the combination of parents would work, since my fiancée's mother was an ultra-organized Italian master chef. Mom decided to try a new recipe—a pasta casserole sure to please their Italian palate, she thought. With smiling confidence, Mom started carrying the dish to the table, only to have it unexpectedly flip from her hands and land upside down on the floor. Without missing a beat, Mom scooped up the pasta that wasn't directly touching the floor, put it back in the dish, and announced with resilience that dinner was ready. True, it was an awkward moment, but as I think back on this experience, I'm thankful Mom carried on with laughter, shrugged off pride, and simply offered what we had with welcoming love.

—Lois

Setting Your Table

We're like Martha with distracted hearts that hold on to home as owners instead of stewards. Stuff, image, and self-imposed standards of prideful perfection enslave hearts that were created to love. But like Martha, we can experience a heart change. We need to let the Bethany dinners instruct us. Martha had an identity problem: She defined her value by her competence. But Martha isn't the only one who suffers from this. Her troubles are mine as well. Her example warns me that I have a problem when I, too, complain, "I'm doing the work by myself." It means I'm leaving Christ out; I've forgotten his kingdom counsel, "Apart from me, you can do nothing." (John 15:5b)

Martha's pre-dinner meltdown reveals a principle as true today as it was then: Identity fuels what we do; what we do reveals identity. In order to move away from our meltdowns and toward Christ's freedom life, we need to ask Christ to open our eyes to who we really are. As we lay down pride and listen to Jesus, our true self in Christ is free to be. His love and call to Martha is his love and call to us. When we listen to Christ, we are set free—carrots or no carrots.

So, who are you? Jesus has the answer. He told his disciples, "No longer do I call you servants. For a servant does not know his master's business. Instead, I have called you friends, for whatever I have learned from my Father I have made known to you." (John 15:15) The most practical, life-changing hospitality habit is to consciously set the table as a friend of Jesus. This simple act of faith transfers ownership of "your" table to him. You will experience Christ as host when you embrace your identity as his cooperative friend.

The first time I heard a speaker use the phrase "cooperative friend of Jesus," I thought of when Jesus asked Peter and John to go ahead to prepare the last meal he ate with the disciples in the upper room: "As you enter the city, a man carrying a jar of water will meet you. Follow him to the house that he enters, and say to the owner of the house, 'the Teacher asks: Where is the guest room, where I may eat the Passover with my disciples?' He will show you a large upper room, all furnished. Make preparations there." (Luke 22:10–12)

The guest room doesn't belong to either Peter or John. What they "own" is glad obedience by doing what the Lord asks them to do. Cutting snips of parsley, buying bread, and pouring wine, they prepare the table for a Passover meal. They don't know Jesus is about to declare the new covenant at this meal; they simply respond to his request as friends.

While they recline, Jesus says, "I have eagerly desired to eat this Passover with you before I suffer." This is equivalent to saying, "I have longingly longed." What vulnerability! This is a tender disclosure of love that shapes the tone and significance of the meal. The disciples' partnership, rewarded by Christ's love, calls us to believe that Christ eagerly longs for fellowship with his friends in the twenty-first century, too.

Hold on to your identity as a cooperative friend of Jesus as if it's your driver's license. When you browse through a Pottery Barn ad, *be attentive to your heart*. Does

The most practical, life-changing hospitality habit is to consciously set the table as a friend of Jesus.

it become restful or restless? Does your response to the marketing world grow or hinder loving relationships celebrated in your home? Think of the times you have put off inviting someone because you were waiting to buy just one more thing or get just one more house project done.

Table life is kingdom living with Jesus as host. "It is for freedom that Christ has set us free. Stand firm then, and do not let yourselves be burdened again by a yoke of slavery." (Galatians 5:1) To this, I can hear the transformed Martha saying, "Yes! Yes!" Let Christ remove the burden of fussy pride. Love your lot; you're a friend of Jesus. Filled with your true identity, you will have room to relax and strength to serve.

Of course, hospitality requires effort and intentionality. I make phone calls, shop for chicken, and wipe water stains off the soup spoons. But the difference between worldly entertaining and table life is that these actions infuse me with freedom as I remember "my" table belongs to Christ.

Here are some ways for living out your identity as a cooperative friend of Jesus:

• *Pursue peace, not perfection, in your preparation.* Practice this by leaving something "undone" on purpose. This might be a little thing no one would notice anyway, but it'll be significant to God as you place pride on the altar. Exchange perfectionism for ten minutes of rest and focus before the guests arrive.

• *Whet your appetite for fellowship, not flattery.* Occasionally, I'll make a world-class loaf of whole-grain bread. On those rare instances of bread euphoria when I've baked an unusually fabulous loaf, I know I've met with host Jesus if I haven't given even one thought to whether guests commented on its taste. (This also holds true for those bad-bread days when I don't bother to fuss over slightly burned crust.) The desire for approval lurks and haunts our human hearts. Silence the "What do you think?" voice by letting Christ own your table.

• *Remember that your "freedom life" blesses others.* I fondly remember greeting a couple at our front door while we were in the midst of a house project. We had decided we weren't going to make our home a keep-out zone during a few months of remodeling. Andrew looked straight over my 5-foot-1-½-inch frame to the two-by-four studs in the background and, like an inspector, made a beeline to the project. The exposed, raw pine studs offered just what our new friend needed to feel at ease.

• *Savor simplicity.* Less is more. There are times for feasting and times for fasting, but most of life is somewhere in between. The fewer entrées we serve, the better the food tastes. It satisfies. With unhurried pleasure, we appreciate the gift more. Think in twos; it was Jesus' style. When he prepared a meal, it was usually fish and bread. What do you enjoy—pizza and Coke, hummus and crackers, spinach salad and focaccia? During our pickle barrel table days, we once served the seminary president a dessert snack of sunflower seeds and a beverage. We knew he watched his diet, and he had requested "something simple." He delighted in munching the seeds, and we got to spend time with a sage.

✦ ✦ ✦ ✦ ✦ ✦ ✦ ✦ ✦ ✦ ✦ ✦

I hope that you, the reader, are discovering the ways God uses our tables to change our hearts. My friend Janet tells her story of a heart change she experienced.

I'll never forget the evening. While traveling in China with my mother, we had the opportunity to have dinner in the home of a local pastor. We arrived at the dirty, aged, run-down apartment building and were escorted up a dingy, garlic-smelling stairway. With an open door, the couple and their nine-year-old son warmly greeted us. As I stepped in, I realized I was standing in a small, single room that served as the living room, dining room, and bedroom. Smaller than my modest-sized living room, it held a bunk bed, piano, small refrigerator, and dresser.

The husband cooked that night and invited me to help make pot stickers. As we stood together in the cramped, greasy kitchen, he patiently showed me how to form the Chinese dumplings. With three other guests present, small plastic chairs, a stool, and the edge of the bunk bed served as seats around a small table. We savored the pot stickers, sipped tea, and munched on a few other snacks as we listened to their stories of coming to Christ. The joy of the Lord filled this home, and we felt loved.

Compared to the home of this Chinese family, my house is a mansion. And yet, I am reluctant to invite others to my home, thinking, it's too small, the carpet is old, I don't have a real dining room, it just isn't good enough. I am rich beyond measure, but how can I be grateful for what God has given me if I am not content? How dare I be ashamed of God's gifts because they aren't as new or big or shiny as someone else's? Thanks to the grace of this Chinese home, I've started to take steps to open my front door.

Taste and See

On the practical side, there are two ways to achieve a "Don't Fuss" dinner—either prepare a simple meal yourself or plan a meal where everyone contributes. One of our favorite contribution meals is Mexican Stack-Up. You provide the meat and tortilla chips, and everyone else brings condiments to stack on top. And if you want to be creative in serving the food, buy terra-cotta-style plastic flowerpot drain dishes. They add a Southwestern look, are inexpensive, and can be used over and over for future parties. I haven't yet met anyone who gets tired of being served Mexican food!

Mexican Stack-Up

2 pounds ground meat
1 large onion, chopped
1 package taco seasoning
½ cup fresh chopped cilantro
1 large can tomatoes
½ cup water
Optional: 1 can refried beans
1 large bag tortilla chips

(Note: This yields 10–12 servings, but prepare according to size of group.)

Sauté meat with onion. Add taco seasoning, cilantro, tomatoes, refried beans, and water, then simmer. Instruct guests to crunch chips on their plates and then add the meat on top. Then have them "stack up" the condiments everyone contributed to the meal, such as shredded lettuce, chopped tomatoes, chopped green onions, sliced avocadoes, shredded cheese, sour cream, chopped olives, salsa, lime slices... and more.

Daily Bread

"So whether you eat or drink or whatever you do, do it all for the glory of God."
(1 Corinthians 10:31)

Prayer

Lord, I confess my fussy pride. Forgive me for times I have focused on possessions and impressions instead of your lavish love for me. Thank you for bringing me to this altar. I transfer ownership of my table to you. It's yours, Lord. Amen

Altar Call

Savoring the presence of Jesus at your table creates a heart that's free to let him be the host.

CHAPTER 6

My Father's Glad Welcome

Jesus the storyteller celebrates a dinner party.

The Jesus Table

Jesus had a tongue like a skillful writer, for his "heart was stirred by a noble theme." (Psalms 45:1) Have you ever asked yourself what inspired Jesus to tell stories? Where did his stories come from? Every word Jesus spoke was the Father's will. The Father's will and Christ's work were one; the Son of God told his stories from the wellspring of an unbroken relationship with his Father.

Jesus woke each morning filled with his Father's love. He did the normal routines of washing and dressing, but unlike us with our fragile and fickle moods, Jesus lived each day with an eternal perspective. After eating breakfast and tying on his sandals, he walked through Judean neighborhoods, seeking the lost while stories brewed in his soul. He longed to draw the religious as well as the outside sinners to His Father's love.

The day came when some Pharisees and teachers of the law complained to Jesus about his eating with sinners. From the vantage point of their sanctimonious legalism, the Pharisees reject Jesus' lifestyle of grace. Maybe a story would open their eyes, Jesus thought. So his story began with the words: "There was a man who had two sons."(Luke 15:11) Nowadays we usually call this story "The

"His father said, quick, bring the finest robe in the house and put it on him. Get a ring for his finger and sandals for his feet. And kill the calf we have been fattening in the pen. We must celebrate with a feast, for this son of mine was dead and now he has returned to life. He was lost but now he's found. So the party began..."

(Luke 15:22–24)

Prodigal Son." But if we sat as Jews at the feet of the storyteller two thousand years ago, our Hebraic ears would have heard it as a shocking story about a father, not a son.

The story unfolded with a son's request: "The younger one said to his father, 'give me my share of the estate.'" (Luke 15:12) The son wanted to leave home, to turn his back on his dad. This request was brazen nonsense to the father and to the religious culture of the ancient Jewish world. Insulting and disrespectful, the words translate, "Drop dead, Dad." When a Jewish son left his father in rebellion, not only did he break the Lord's commandment "Honor your father and mother," but he also left his whole community. Shame hung like a millstone around the father's neck. As days passed and news reached home that his son ate with swine in pagan pastures, the father's shame rotted into a monstrous sorrow.

I've often wondered about Jesus' emotion as he told this story. Think of the sound of his voice and the look on his face. His sorrow over a son rebelling was the reason he embraced his Father's plan for the cross. Perhaps the Pharisees noticed Jesus' brown eyes welling with tears. Imagine how such tenderness might have caught the Pharisees off guard. Tears can do that. The outrage and indignation at the son's conduct may not have been the only unrest in the crowd, for perhaps some of the religious elite were fearful Jesus was taking their own hearts to a place they didn't want to go. Jesus called it grace.

The next scene of Jesus' story beamed grace into the pit of the prodigal's despair. Jesus said, "He came to his senses." (Luke 15:17) In other words, the son saw his true self and desperate need, perhaps praying, "I'm a mess and alone, God—help me!" Longing and desolation turned the son toward home. The son knew he needed home, but he feared the fallout. He knew his father had every right to punish him or even banish him from the house. So his plan was to come disguised as a hired hand; it covered his shame while leaving a back door open.

But Jesus rocked the Pharisees with the father's response: "But while he was still a long way off, his father saw him and was filled with compassion for him; he ran to his son, threw his arms around him and kissed him." (Luke 15:20) This one line in Jesus' story was the golden thread of truth and grace—only the father could restore the separation. The father ran to embrace his son with forgiveness. Surprisingly, his unrestrained love ignored all Jewish protocol. Older Jewish men didn't run; it was undignified because it required pulling up garments and exposing bare legs. Jesus' story implied that the son returned in broad daylight. No doubt villagers watched the father with eyes of judgment.

But with unselfconscious, extravagant love—lavishing the son with kisses, a new robe, and sandals—the father declared a dinner party. "Bring the fattened calf and kill it." (Luke 15:23) Set the table. Roast the meat. A fatted calf plated enough meals for one hundred people. It was time for a community celebration. It was time to celebrate the miracle that his son was back from the dead. Love resurrected the lost. Joy broke out. The calf roasted. The neighbors came. The music began.

But there was one person missing from the party: the dutiful elder brother. He hunkered in the shadows—proud, sulky, angry, distant, and disrespectful. But the father's love embraced him, too. Always the pursuer, the father left the party, ignoring Hebrew custom once more, by going to his elder son. Love poured from his lips: "My son, you are always with me, and everything I have is yours." (Luke 1:31)

Jesus the storyteller heard those same affectionate words "my son" at his own baptism. He knew the powerful connection of receiving the Father's affirmation. The Father love that poured over him in the Jordan River flowed through his lips as a storyteller. Jesus wanted the Pharisees listening to his story to step out of their dark brooding so they could also come to the Father's love.

He wanted everyone to be at the party. The words Jesus meticulously put in the mouth of the parable father reveal what love does: The Father told the elder son, "We had to celebrate and be glad…" (Luke 15:32) The father's love suffered, but ultimately, the father's love was joy. Joy is the essence of the father's heart for a repentant son. Love shows off joy. Love spills joy on the person being loved. The father didn't stuff his joy or quench his instinct to celebrate. As the father delighted in his younger son's repentance, he also stood face to face with the elder, sulky son, pleading he come home to the party.

✦ ✦ ✦ ✦ ✦ ✦ ✦ ✦ ✦ ✦ ✦ ✦ ✦ ✦

Scripture records forty parables that Jesus told, and this parable is the longest. It's just my opinion, but I think this story was Jesus' favorite. Jesus went to bed that night, satisfied he told every detail that would best portray the Father's happy, welcoming love. And when he got up the next morning to have breakfast, perhaps he sat at the table, anticipating how this story of the Father's welcome would transform our homes, too, two thousand years later. "Because of Christ and our trust in him, we can now come fearlessly into his presence, assured of his glad welcome." (Ephesians 3:12, *NLT*)

Oh Dear!

My husband and I were hosting a dinner for four expat couples from our church—all Americans living near Lausanne, Switzerland. Midmeal, I left the table to replenish the platter of baked parmesan bread. One of the wives followed me to help. We chatted in the kitchen as I was loading the platter. Suddenly both of us stopped talking, our breath taken away by a revolting sight: a fat, hairy caterpillar, encrusted in cheese, was baked firmly onto a slice of the bread. I was horrified. *I felt exposed in this obvious hosting flaw. She was horrified, too, to be honest; however, she didn't overreact. She was more than gracious. She didn't ignore the caterpillar's presence (how could she?) or the reality of my imperfection. Recognizing both, she chose to walk with me through what steps to take next—yes,* definitely dump all the bread, *but no, don't tell anyone else. She moved me from being paralyzed in dismay to being able to rejoin the table in a calm state, so I could be open and present to my guests. (I did notice at the end of the meal, though, that this wife left her bread uneaten on her plate—smart move!)*

—*Lisa*

Finding Your Table

Jesus' story *insisted* on a table. The father's love required a fatted calf. Minimal provision for a starving son would not do; this meal was about the pure happiness of father love. "We had to celebrate and be glad!" *We* had to celebrate. This word underscores the power of the father's relationship to his family. The father's joy pulled family together. He thought communally. That's because the father knew his own heart. This father's love represents the Heavenly Father's love, which is pure and full and free. It was inconceivable for this father to calculate his invitations to the party based on merit. The party wasn't to honor earned favor; it was to celebrate with one and all how love scooped up a wayward son come home.

So we must ask ourselves how our own tables celebrate God's glad welcome. What might we be missing? We need to dig deeper than our busyness and crammed calendars to answer the question. It's more about an attitude to cultivate. Do you connect your practice of hospitality with the picture of God the Father running toward you to take you in his arms of love and then host a party for you? No, I'm not asking if you hug everybody who comes to your house. I'm asking how God's embracing love motivates you to share your table.

Years ago, my Heavenly Father called me to the feast of forgiveness. I responded in repentance; Jesus took my sin, cast it into hell, and placed me in his kingdom. Angels sang. I am forever God's child, a daughter of King Jesus. Salvation is not fiction; it is a true story based on faith in Christ. Millions have come to this table. *Every meal shared among believers is designed to represent and celebrate his glad welcome of forgiven sinners coming home.* Ever so simply, at every meal, God invites us to remember when our hearts first turned to receive Jesus' love.

God is so kind to place the shared meal as a formative accessible reminder of his joy over us.

But we forget. We forget our kingdom identity and true inheritance. We forget we're extravagantly loved today. Our troubles and fears and transgressions are like viruses that dull our senses and disconnect our hearts from God's happiness. It's like forgetting the wonder of a child's birth on a colicky day. This "identity amnesia" often has us wandering the kingdom, not knowing there's a cupboard with food and a table to enjoy with our brothers and sisters. God is so kind to place the shared meal as a formative, accessible reminder of his joy over us.

Another way we miss practicing the glad welcome of the table is with disappointing and broken relationships. We hurt others, and we've been hurt. We sin against others, and we sulk behind shadows. Even just an inkling of pride separates us from one another. Sometimes we just disappear, hoping no one notices our absence.

We fail to honor the incentive table life offers in calling us to keep short accounts with our brothers and sisters. God made families to eat together, but when was the last time you thought of sharing a meal with someone in the body of Christ with whom you had a misunderstanding? Sounds scary, doesn't it? Even though we are family (just like the younger and elder brother), we pretend that connection doesn't matter.

I'm not suggesting the first step in mending a broken relationship is sipping lattes together. Repenting, restoring, and rebuilding mutual understanding requires heart work. It takes time. Sometimes we need a third-party peacemaker to help us. But imagine the robust health spreading in the living church if believers practiced repentance at the party God provides—a shared meal. This is the radical, yet practical faith the Heavenly Father yearns for his children. He doesn't force feed, but he watches, calls, offers, and waits.

Before moving on to Setting Your Table, consider another factor that can trick us into forfeiting the benefits of celebrating God's glad welcome at our tables: fear of loss. We are a mobile, transient nation. People come and go. A generation cycle feels more like three or four years, not twenty-one. So we're tempted to put on our self-protective armor with the cynical question, "Why bother reaching out to them? They'll probably not even be around next year." As I once flipped through my journal of those who've come to our table, a wave of sadness caught me off guard—many who had come are now gone. I felt discouragement and a smidgeon of futility...until I let God give me a new perspective.

Lifestyle Check: Do I have a broken relationship that needs a table?

Heart Check: How does God's glad welcoming love motivate me to share my table?

Setting Your Table

Big things come in little packages. Is there anything bigger than being forgiven with glad welcome by God? And the table is the little, practical place where the big love of God celebrates. Some days I don't feel particularly close to God, but I set the table by faith, anyway. By the end of the meal, I've made a connection with God's love through the life of a guest. On other days, God's love is very real to me, and I'm humbled that my table is a place to remember and share it.

In the previous section, we discussed how "forgetful" we are. We forget divine forgiveness. We forget we're God's children. And we forget to forgive. Forgetting costs us our happiness. The cure for forgetfulness is an active commitment to remember. And there's no better place than the table to remember how much God loves us.

Putting a favorite food on the table for a child you disciplined earlier in the day connects the child's heart to God's forgiveness.

Make a commitment to view your table as a remembrance of God's glad welcome. This isn't an arbitrary, artificial connection; it's God's deliberate design. He knows remembering the need to eat is exceedingly practical. I've never said, "Oops, I forgot to eat today!" I've decided to skip a meal on rare occasions. I've fasted. But I've never *forgotten* to eat. I'm fascinated by the association Jesus intentionally made with meals and remembering. When he spoke the new covenant to his disciples, he chose the context of a meal and said, "Do this in remembrance of me." (Luke 22:19) He said that for *our* benefit, not his! He knew we're inherently forgetful, so he picked the repetitive need of a meal to remind us of his unfailing love. Just as he gave the Lord's Supper to the church, he gives us tables at home to spread the happiness of forgiveness.

The table can be a place of forgiveness and welcome for families. Putting a favorite food on the table for a child you disciplined earlier in the day connects the child's heart to God's forgiveness. It says, "I love you." If she's a watermelon fan, cut her a sweet slice decorated with a happy face made with the seeds. Saying grace at dinner matters. We don't lose God's love if we forget to say thank you, but remembering to say grace reinforces our identity as children lavishly loved by God. Listening to preschoolers pray at the table always makes us smile; it's so simple and authentic. Our joy in those moments gives us a taste of the Father's joy over us. As children get older, sometimes self-consciousness kicks in when saying grace. Parents, don't force children to verbalize prayer, but instead lead your families in giving thanks.

Have your children ever heard your welcome-home-to-God story? My mom was in her nineties when I first heard her describe holding her daddy's hand while skipping home from church, full of joy in accepting Jesus. Set aside a dinner to tell your story.

This sharing also works when friends gather at the table. Every believer has a glad welcome story. One of the simplest questions to ask at the table is, "Tell us the story of how you came to Christ." Not everyone may share. But it's amazing how hearing just one story points us all back to the joy of God's welcome. Remembering God's glad welcome *for ourselves* changes our perspective toward *others* who come to our tables. We see a brother or sister, not a stranger. It's another discovery of the table as an altar. As the apostle Paul wrote, "Be transformed by the renewing of your mind." (Romans 12:2)

I had an experience when the physical act of coming to the table opened my eyes. It is a picture I've never forgotten. I was standing at our table—all 5-foot-1-½-inches of me—and to my right was a strapping 6-foot-8-inch man. I craned my neck to look at him and wondered if I should have made extra soup. As we pulled the folding chairs out and squeezed into our small dining space, the dramatic height differences were a bit comical—a mighty giant, miniature me, and everyone else in between.

But then a visual transformation came to view: We sat down. The table invited us in. We humbled ourselves to the call of the table and shared a common need—dinner. Our individual uniqueness didn't dissolve, but our common life highlighted grace as we faced one another at the table, now sitting eye to eye. This dinner reminded me that eating together celebrates a faith reality: In Jesus Christ, we are all provided forgiveness of sins. The cross of Christ is level ground. We are all sinners saved by grace, extravagantly loved by God. The next time you sit at the table, look at the others eating with you as people extravagantly loved by God—whether it's your spouse, who forgot to pick up the milk at the grocery store, or a new neighbor you're getting to know. You'll enjoy them more.

The next time you sit at the table, look at others eating with you as people extravagantly loved by God.

But I confess, sometimes I have judged others harshly, superficially, and hastily. I once extended an invitation by phone, and from one brief conversation I decided I had just invited a cranky curmudgeon. An "oh no" washed over me like a dose of vinegar, but my judgment proved wrong. By the end of the meal, I realized underneath the crusty personality was a man who loved Jesus in his own quirky way. I needed this meal to remind me of the Father's love that forgives my pride.

We're all prone to be picky about what we eat. We're picky about with *whom* we eat, too. We tend to limit table life to people who think, play, spend, age, and look just like us. We forfeit the richness of having a feeble, bent-over saint sit at the table with a young punk because we cling to the untested assumption that the generation gap is unbridgeable. The truth is, choosing to live the glad welcome life will make your table a sacred place to discover Jesus in every generation. Give it a try.

We also set our glad welcome tables with God when we offer them as places to restore relationships. Have you ever extended a dinner invitation as a way to heal a broken connection? Sometimes our invitations aren't accepted, but the offer still honors Christ. Romans 15:7 is the gospel standard: "Accept one another as Christ has accepted you." Expressing words of forgiveness and confession are essential to all conflict. Humbly giving a simple gift makes forgiveness tangible, and that gift just might be a meal. Jesus himself taught the kingdom significance of offering a cup of cold water.

All God's people have conflict. I remember when my husband and I felt anguish over a broken relationship with another couple in the church. The pain lasted for months. It invited us to a season of self-examination, confession, and prayerful waiting. Slowly, God did healing work between us. When the time was ripe to rebuild the relationship, we met at an office in the church building. The setting was okay, but I thought the office atmosphere would lack personal warmth. We were getting together to bless relationship, not hold a business meeting. So I brought an antique glass pitcher of ice water and perched orange slices on the rim of four glasses. Our coming together created holy ground as a common need—a sip of water—calmed our nervousness.

Just as God's glad welcome creates a bond of belonging, so the living church is a place to belong. But how do we keep setting our tables when people move away? Change is inevitable. We must choose to practice gratitude by acknowledging every shared meal is a gift of grace. It's not a right, it's a privilege. Heaven will gather God's people; but on earth, God grows his kingdom with seed that scatters. God's glad welcome keeps our hearts and homes open to tomorrow's opportunity of making our tables a place to belong.

If or when it's your turn to move, make your table a place to savor the bonds of grace. The whole family of God is blessed when we honor our unity in Christ. Devote the meal to a time for sharing how your faith has grown while being a part of the church family. From laughter to tears, cherish the memories. Verbalize gratitude. Pray together. God's glad welcome never changes, and someday we will all sit together at the marriage supper of the Lamb.

Taste and See

Perhaps there is no other food that best symbolizes Jesus' glad welcome than bread. There's nothing like the aroma of bread baking to welcome friends and family home. I prefer going the whole-grain route in its pure form, but many people aren't accustomed to that heavier taste. Also, if you're a novice at bread baking, you'll most likely get a fuller rise by mixing both whole-grain and white flour. Here's a great recipe, but don't hesitate to throw in some extra nutritional ingredients, such as millet, oatmeal, or rye.

Honey Wheat Bread

3 cups water, slightly warmed
½ cup canola oil
½ cup honey
1 tablespoon dry yeast
1 tablespoon salt
2 cups unbleached white flour
8–9 cups whole-wheat flour

Warm the water, then add oil, honey, yeast, salt, and white flour. Let sit a while, then add whole-wheat flour. Dough should be slightly sticky, but not hard to handle. Avoid drying out dough with too much flour. Knead until smooth and elastic, about 10 minutes. Place in a large, greased bowl. Cover and leave in a warm, draft-free place until doubled in size. Punch down. Form into 2 loaves, place in 2 greased pans. Cover and rise 1 hour. Bake 350°F for 40–45 minutes.

(Tip: Use an instant-read thermometer to test doneness. It should register at least 180°F.)

Daily Bread

"Accept one another, then, just as Christ accepted you, in order to bring praise to God." (Romans 15:7)

Prayer

Abba, Father, to receive your unfailing love is my heart's true joy. Thank you. May my table be a place to cherish bonds of love. In Jesus' name, amen.

Altar Call

Savoring the welcoming presence of Jesus at your table creates a heart filled with joy.

CHAPTER 7

A Place of Grace

Jesus the Savior eats with outsiders.

The Jesus Table

Rabbis taught while they walked, maximizing every opportunity to teach about God. And the road along the Sea of Galilee was often Jesus' classroom. But neither the crowd walking with him nor the view of the water kept him from noticing the need of just one person. On one occasion, he sees Levi, a tax collector, sitting in a tollbooth, smug and confident. A tax collector's reputation is like a prostitute's—nothing but shame. Jews despise everything Levi represents: deceit, extortion, and abusive power. They see him as a traitor, outsider, and religiously unclean. They reject him and want nothing to do with him.

Now imagine the crowd's shock when Jesus actually stops to talk to Levi. He looks into Levi's eyes and says, "Follow me." (Matthew 9:9) What a strange invitation! In the traditional rabbinical ways, only a select few "righteous students" were invited to follow a rabbi to the next level of instruction. Scripture doesn't provide the entire dialogue between Jesus and Levi. They may have talked several times before, or maybe Levi had eavesdropped on the teacher whenever he walked by. But this time, the "numbers guy" lets down his guard in the presence of Jesus. Jesus offers grace—if Levi confesses his sins, he will receive the gift of forgiveness.

"WHILE JESUS WAS HAVING DINNER AT MATTHEW'S HOUSE, MANY TAX COLLECTORS AND 'SINNERS' CAME AND ATE WITH HIM AND HIS DISCIPLES. WHEN THE PHARISEES SAW THIS, THEY ASKED HIS DISCIPLES, 'WHY DOES YOUR TEACHER EAT WITH TAX COLLECTORS AND SINNERS?'"

(Matthew 9:10)

In this unexpected encounter, Levi honestly looks at his own heart. His addictions and deceptions weigh heavier than the lure of Herod's treasury. Sin is his misery. So he stands up. Fidgeting inside his booth, the competent tax thief steps away from coin stacks and accounting sheets to come to Jesus. Levi believes Jesus and receives a new life. Stepping out of the bondage of sin into God's love changes the man and his name. Levi becomes Matthew, which means "gift of God."

As days and weeks pass, Matthew's new life doesn't quiet criticism from the community. The poor still despise him, and the religious still condemn him. But Matthew knows salvation is the real deal—he's a redeemed son, a prodigal who returned to the Father's love. The ledger of sin's account is wiped out by grace, and the evil ambition to hoard transforms into a holy ambition to love. He left his idols, but still has his friends.

What better way for Matthew to love his tax-collecting friends and other outcasts than to invite them to have dinner with Jesus and his disciples! His wealth enables him to plan a fabulous meal worthy of a write-up in the *Capernaum Journal*'s food section. But the real news of the day is that Matthew's new heart views his table with new eyes. His table belongs to Christ. His new heart delights to live the good news of grace around the intimacy of the table.

Matthew's hospitality offers the happy overflow of his forgiven heart, though he doesn't calculate the kerfuffle his dinner provokes. Pharisees gripe about Jesus eating with Matthew's sinner friends. Eating with social outcasts means ceremonial defilement. As a rabbi, Jesus ought to know better! Contempt reddens their self-righteous faces. But instead of confronting Jesus directly, they interrogate his disciples, "Why does your teacher eat with tax collectors and 'sinners'?" (Matthew 9:11)

Then Jesus steps in. He doesn't let the Pharisees blow out the oil lanterns at the dinner party. This table represents the reason the Messiah came. With rabbinic authority, he counters their protest by saying, "It is not the healthy who need a doctor, but the sick. But go and learn what this means: 'I desire mercy, not sacrifice.' For I have not come to call the righteous, but sinners." (Matthew 9:12)

The Pharisees don't understand Jesus' place at the table. He doesn't eat with sinners because he winks at sin; he eats with them because they need grace. Jesus doesn't fear external contamination; he lives to love sinners. So it makes sense to eat turnips with the truants. Craig L. Blomberg, author of *Contagious Holiness*, describes it best: Jesus isn't at risk of catching the disease of sin because he eats with sinners; sinners are at risk of being drawn to grace by eating with Jesus.[1]

The Pharisees don't understand Matthew's table is for them, too. Jesus never stops offering grace. He says to them, "Go and learn," which is a rabbinic formula they know well. It means *go back to the scriptures*. They are law experts, and it's time to take another look. If Jesus' words carry a tinge of needling humor, it is for an ultimate good—to draw the Pharisees to the light of God's perfect law. "I desire mercy, not sacrifice" (Hosea 6:6) means God wants the heart. Jesus knows his Father's sadness over the Pharisees' spiritual blindness. Their external rituals of temple worship are lifeless without confessing their own need for grace.

Matthew's heart surrendered to God's grace. God pursues the heart because he created us to be wholly his and because we can't be whole without him. Man can't clean his own heart, no matter how many rules he keeps. "Go and learn" calls the Pharisees—and us all—to grace.

✦ ✦ ✦ ✦ ✦ ✦ ✦ ✦ ✦ ✦ ✦ ✦ ✦

Receiving God's glad welcome creates an inner change, and Christian hospitality is the ripple of grace that flows outward to others. Nearly all the New Testament commands to practice hospitality are about believers opening their homes *to other believers.* This priority makes perfect sense when I think of my eagerness to work my way through crowds at the airport in order to get to my daughter's house in Houston in time to eat Christmas dinner at her table. It's a family thing. It's love. We want to be together.

The church as a family is precious to God, too. Our identity as brothers and sisters in Christ is mentioned over two hundred times in the New Testament. Hospitality isn't for making the church an exclusive insider club, but for growing the church into a winsome family of grace.

But just as we're called to open our homes to other believers, Jesus also calls us to live the grace life of our tables *beyond our church family ties.* I wish we knew more about Matthew's dinner. How many guests came? Did Matthew ask Jesus to give thanks for the food in front of his irreverent friends? Who did Jesus sit next to? What did they talk about? Did he get up to help serve wine? Did he rave about a delicacy he had never tasted before? My curiosities fade compared to the beauty that Christ simply delighted in the occasion. Religion likely wasn't the topic of the party, but faith was the reason for it. Jesus was not defensive or jumpy about eating a meal outside religious boundaries. Rather, he came to engage in real life—the intimate setting of a home. What's more natural than a Friday night with new friends?

Grace and truth *partied*, and the partygoers couldn't ignore Matthew's newfound faith. He was a changed man, and Jesus was the friend who changed him. The other guests may have arrived curious, suspicious, indifferent, or clueless, but because of Matthew's generosity, that night they got to eat dinner with God.

Finding Your Table

If, like Matthew, you've come to see your need for Christ, then his amazing grace has transformed your table into a place for outsiders to experience grace. Is it? The word *outsider* is not a label devaluing a person's worth; it's a description of separation. It describes a condition of being disconnected or isolated. Most of us knew by kindergarten what it feels like to be an outsider. Someone made fun of us because we didn't have the right brand of shoes, and we felt left out. The religious elite of Jesus' day hounded sinners for being outside God's moral perfection. They refused to offer hope, but Jesus' mission to save sinners was about bringing outsiders to grace and into his Father's family.

We're all born into the world disconnected from God due to sin. Matthew left a tax booth to come to Jesus; I left a pew at the end of a church service to come to Jesus. Two different pathways, but the same magnanimous gift was received— God's forgiveness. Matthew didn't worry about labels. The sheer joy of grace compelled him to invite his friends to have a dinner with Jesus.

The more I think about Matthew, the more I know I should be like him, but Matthew's table gets under my skin. It's a wake-up call. He let grace reach out to all those in his sphere, including the outsider. Sometimes Pharisaical blind spots keep me from offering grace to the "others" in my everyday life.

I'm reminded of a time my husband and I ate at a Tibetan restaurant. As we nibbled on perfectly steamed yak dumplings, I looked across the tiny, square, sparse room and noticed two people eating their dumplings. Then my appetite soured. With that one glance, I made judgments about their lifestyle. I put them in a box and inwardly fretted that they were "spoiling" my meal. My judgment lured me into becoming judgmental. My heart shifted from evaluating to sinning. I was caught again in the icy-cold glacier of spiritual pride. Then I silently prayed, "Lord, have mercy."

Grace flows freely out of a humbled heart. God's breath of mercy melted my sin, and I began to feel the Spirit's love and compassion change my perspective. I began to pray a blessing for the diners across the room. I realized they were enjoying dinner, too. They were partaking in a gift God provided, whether they loved the Giver or not. As we drove home, we talked about sin, forgiveness, and grace. This experience humbled me and warned me that I could easily become one of those Pharisees crashing Matthew's party with contempt. But it also taught me that when I turn away from my Pharisaical categorizing and remember God's glad welcome, he opens my eyes and empowers me to live like Matthew.

Matthew began by opening his home to the relationship sphere with which he was most familiar: his coworkers and friends. It was the first ripple of grace flowing outward, but not the last. Grace kept doing deep work in Matthew's heart. He stepped out of the tax booth, trusting Jesus' claim to forgive sin. Later, he became an eye witness to the incalculable price for grace at Christ's Crucifixion. The more he understood grace, the more he wanted to invite outsiders into it. The last words Matthew heard Jesus say before ascending to his Father in heaven were, "Go and make disciples of all nations." (Mark 28:19) The ripple of grace is still on the move.

What keeps us from opening our homes to outsiders? Matthew's table encourages us to examine two obstacles. The first obstacle is a *judgmental spirit*, which focuses on the offense of the sin over the value of the person made in God's image. This is what the Pharisees stumbled over. Take time to know yourself: Do you tend to allow a person's dubious reputation or different appearance keep you from offering a taste of Christ's grace? Do you react to your neighbor's crabbiness by

The more he understood grace, the more he wanted to invite outsiders into it.

withholding your own practical kindness? Does your value for order, quiet, and cleanliness keep you from inviting the neighbor kids for cookies and milk? What habits and judgments quell the ripple of grace within you?

The second potential obstacle is *reluctance to take risks.* Though Matthew's guests were his longstanding friends, he had become a new person. He didn't know how they would respond to his new life or to Jesus. There was the possibility that he would lose some friendships after the last bite of dessert. But he took the risk for the sake of love.

What feels risky to you? What are you self-conscious or intimidated about? Is it what someone might bring into your home—a careless tongue, smelly cigarettes? Does it make you nervous that someone may bring a bottle of wine, when you don't even own a corkscrew? Do you feel uncomfortable about making an outward expression of your faith, such as praying before the meal, visible to your guests?

Finding your table is not about finding outsiders, it's about finding yourself. It's about identifying *your issues* so you can ask Jesus to overcome your fears so the ripple of grace is free to flow. For example, fearing how others may respond to an invitation may stem from the need for control and approval. Allowing fears to control us keeps us from loving. People are God's greatest treasure, and he wants us to appreciate and enjoy the unique gifts others bring to the table. And even an outsider to grace most likely won't mind if you thank God for the hamburgers on the grill. Relax. Remember, grace works.

Oh Dear!

As a newlywed, my doable menus consisted mostly of sandwiches, tough pork chops, and a "gourmet" dish I copied from a magazine called "Beans and Weenies Waikiki" (pork 'n' beans, chopped hot dogs, and canned pineapple tidbits heated in a pan). We had moved to a brand-new town, and we were excited when a couple in the community accepted our invitation to dinner. After some consternation about what to serve our first-time guests, I decided pork chops would give the best impression that I knew how to cook. Much to my horror and naiveté, I discovered shortly before their arrival that our guests were Jewish and that Jewish people don't eat pork! But much to my relief, they were very gracious and explained that they would be happy to eat whatever I had prepared.

—Karen

Lifestyle Check: Do I invite the outsider to my home for a meal?

Heart Check: In what ways do I allow a judgmental spirit keep me from sharing meals with outsiders to grace?

Setting Your Table

Like Matthew's party, our open doors and prepared tables are opportunities to spread the love of Christ to those who don't yet know him. But as we set our tables with God, let's keep in mind the manner or spirit with which I believe Matthew welcomed his friends. I don't think they felt like they were his evangelism project. No one wants to be treated like a project. When Jesus gave the church the command to go make disciples, he really gave us the mandate to serve. Serving is the essence of hospitality.

I'll never forget the time I felt like a project. We were visiting the ancient city of Ephesus. Our personal guide marched through the marble ruins as if he were late for an appointment, yet he urged us to stop and watch some skilled rug makers. The light started to dawn—he was their business partner. We reluctantly entered the store, but then two handsome Turkish men gladly welcomed us and offered stout coffee, spiced tea, or Coca-Cola. "How nice," I thought. We chatted while waiting for our beverages. As we stood there, several women nimbly combed and clipped wool on looms with mesmerizing fluidity. I was fascinated. And then the sales pitch began. Dozens of gorgeous rugs were unrolled. We curled our toes, enjoying their cushiony pelt and marvelous colors, but we weren't shopping for rugs.

Once the sellers realized we weren't buying, their former glad welcome became a disgruntled huff. Of course, I realize they had a product to sell. But I felt used. I wasn't naïve—I knew our visit to the warehouse was about commerce, not community. *But my heart readily registered the difference between their reception and their sendoff.* By the end, their welcome felt enormously inauthentic. This experience counseled me: A genuine glad welcome always honors the dignity of personhood. It doesn't push, demand, or manipulate.

Hospitality—and all the fun ideas, helpful reminders, and spontaneous opportunities for opening our homes—must flow from gospel authenticity. In other words, like Matthew, we mustn't sell the gospel; we must live the gospel. We proclaim the gospel with every bite of food, kindness, and respectful conversation. We wait. We don't live for the "sell"; we live for the Savior. We don't make people our projects; we make our homes havens where the contagious wonder of grace reveals the truth of Jesus. Here are some practical steps toward that goal.

1. *Everybody needs Jesus, but ask yourself, who needs the gift of your table?* Distractions, information overload, and "compassion fatigue" can sap our focus. My energy returns when I remember God is sustaining the universe, while I just live in my Minneapolis suburb. Limits are a gift reminding me to let God be God. They free me to respond to my "little important world" with heart, mind, and hands.

It's been years since David and Kathy lived in England as expatriates. But time and the distance of an ocean hasn't erased their vivid memory of Carlos sitting at their table. They had connected with Carlos when he visited their international church and met Matthew, a young man from Australia who lived with David and Kathy. Introductions led to a dinner invitation. Making room for one extra place at the table excited their grade-school daughters, Emily and Katie. They jabbered nonstop while Carlos quietly listened. After dinner, David left the table to tuck the girls in bed. It was then that Carlos asked Kathy in amazement, "Do your children always eat with you?" He told his story of growing up in a Columbian political

We don't make people our projects; we make our homes havens where the contagious wonder of grace reveals the truth about Jesus.

home fraught with danger, fear, and isolation. Instead of having the blessing of table life with his parents, he lived with a twenty-four-hour bodyguard. He came to England for his safety, and God brought him to a table of grace.

For Wendy and Mark, the grace life they receive is the grace life they give away. They happily remember the faces of boys from the inner city who hopped in their van to come to their house for dinner after some heart-throbbing games of basketball with their sons. These unkempt, neglected youth drank in their love, consumed nutritious food, and learned basic table manners because Wendy and Mark live the grateful life of grace.

2. Listen to what God has put in you. Ellen's heart beats for women in prison. For months, she went to visit an inmate in the controlled environment of barbed wire, watchful guards, and a glass-lined visiting room. She faithfully brought the outlandish love of Jesus to this sequestered place. Ellen told me, "During my routine visits, we never had the opportunity to share even a cup of water. But finally the day came when we could sit together and not be separated by the glass visitation wall. I couldn't believe the joy I felt by sharing a cup of water with her. It surprised me with a qualitatively different sense of connection."

God has given Deanna a deep desire to reach out to Asian women—it runs right over her reserved Canadian temperament. She wonders why God planted her in a lawn-mowing suburb and not a diverse city. But demographics change. The first time we went to the local farmers' market, her face beamed like a stack of ripe red tomatoes: Behind each vegetable stall stood a beautiful, hardworking woman from Thailand, Vietnam, or Laos. Years ago, Deanna started building a friendship with Nina, a Taiwanese woman she met during postgraduate studies. They both shared a passion for the challenges of academia. Eventually, job opportunities took them in separate directions, but their friendship was nurtured with letters, phone calls, and reunions of table life. Twenty years after their friendship first began, Nina called Deanna to tell her she had come to faith in Christ.

What fascinates *you*? Do you dream of traveling abroad, but can't afford it? Let the world come to your table. Dive into the adventure of hosting a foreign exchange student. We've done it in opposite seasons of life—during the diapering days and during the empty nest. The joy of new relationships far outweighs the adjustments and sacrifices. Ida and Dennis are truly like our daughter and son. Just weeks after Ida arrived from Denmark, she went with us to Wes and Judy's house for dinner. The laughter and love of that night was the prelude to Ida asking on the drive home her first question about grace. She was hungry for God and gladly went to church. Ida loved our two-year-old, ate crispy Spanish cheese pie at our table, and at the end of the year, she returned to Denmark loving Jesus.

Years later, we welcomed Dennis, the German boy who taught us that every-thing tastes better with cream—from stroganoff to crème brûlée! A gregarious guy, Dennis spent scads of time with friends, but he always came home for dinner. We treasured every fabulous conversation and energetic inquiry. Dennis returned to Germany convinced Jesus called him to be a pastor. And that's what he is doing today.

The ripple of grace is on the move. Coming-to-Jesus stories don't necessarily happen every time you open your door, but every open door offers his grace. Who or what does your heart beat for? Our passions pull us "out there," from the marketplace, to the gym, to the soccer field. But when we invite those "out there" to join us "in here"—where we eat and sleep, rest and create, laugh and listen—God uses our personal spaces as sanctuaries to bring others nearer to him.

3. *Love your story and pass it on.* Your life story is unique—who you are and where you came from. Your story contains the remarkable power to touch others' hearts. It's God's way to prepare and equip you to reach out to others. Nancy's story tells this well:

When I was a teenager, my friends were always welcome in our home. Mom would make warm banana bread and serve it with milk and a smile. She was a single parent, struggling to make ends meet. The simple act of cooking and baking allowed her to share what she did have.

I think one reason I love to cook and bake is because it brings people together. My preparation is an invitation to a shared experience. My teenage children often tell their new friends, "My mom will try to feed you." Sometimes we go out to eat with their friends. We have fun, but it's different because I miss the preparation and ambiance of home. At home, we eat a meal we've prepared together. Yes, I get them involved—pouring the milk and clearing the table afterward. This says, "Welcome, you are part of our family."

I remember one of my daughter's friends who often ate with us since her parents worked late and she didn't want to go home to an empty house. One time, my daughter and I sat at the kitchen counter with her and talked about her parents splitting up. Her sadness and uncertainty shone through her eyes. As the three of us sat eating grilled cheese and tomato soup, I shared my own childhood experience of parents divorcing. I knew the pain.

When my daughter started high school, a whole new set of friends have come to the house. I'm learning that when I serve teens barbeque wings and chips, I am sending them the message that they are worthy of my time and effort. Among her friends one time was a teenage mom who brought her baby. I offered to take her baby so she

could relax and enjoy the meal. Her eyes said it all: "Yes, I could really use a break!"
As I walked the baby, I prayed for him and the teens around my table.

Welcoming teens into my home has enriched my life. Across the kitchen counter,
I've had conversations I never had with my mom at that age. I've had the oppor-
tunity to listen, guide, and encourage. I've learned not to get stressed when things
don't go as planned. By simply offering a snack, soda, or a "stay longer for dinner"
invitation, I get to be a part of what God is doing.

4. *Live out loud your celebrations.* Everyone celebrates: Athletes give high-fives.
Graduates fling mortarboards. Seven-year-olds wake up with gap-toothed grins on
their birthdays. Celebrations are like a break in the clouds on a rainy day—they
invite us to breathe in the good air. Wholesome celebration is winsome; it's good
for us.

Faith celebrations in your home can be natural, nonthreatening connections
with neighbors and friends who may not have personal faith of their own. Faith
celebrations blend the authenticity of your faith with the currency of common
celebration. Almost everyone enjoys Christmas carols and creamy cheesecake with
cherry sauce, no matter what their faith background may be. The cultural wars
(such as "Merry Christmas" versus "Happy Holidays") come to a halt when you
open your door to exhausted, debt-ridden shoppers for refreshment, some remi-
niscing about childhood Christmas traditions, and a few minutes to hear someone
share the story of Christmas. Check out Christmasgatherings.com for more ideas.
Just as the Food Network cooks have websites to empower you in your kitchen, the
Christmas Gathering website will empower you to see how timely and delightful
a Christmas party can be to make another ripple of grace. It just may be the best
Christmas gift you ever give.

Oh Dear!

We were celebrating a
birthday with two other
families. I wanted to
make the cake fun, so I
came up with the idea to
stick six sparklers into the
cake and light them. The
cake was an awesome
display of colorful sparks,
and everyone oohed and
ahed. But when the
sparklers were done and
the smoke cleared, the
cake was totally covered
with black pieces of ash.
The kids tried to scrape off
the "dirty" frosting, but
the cake even tasted like
the sparklers smelled—
terrible! But our laughter
was worth the burn.
—Deb

Almost everyone enjoys Christmas carols and creamy cheesecake with cherry sauce no matter what their faith background may be.

This world of bad news needs good news. And as Pastor John Piper writes, "The gospel is the best news, because what it reports can make people happy forever."[2] When Susan told me her faith story, I was drawn into the evidence that the world is watching how we live in our homes. Susan looked like she had it all—a gregarious personality, a gorgeous home, and a handsome, hardworking husband. But her marriage was crumbling, and her lonely heart yearned for peace. Susan noticed her Christian neighbors frequently having friends over for dinner. From her living room window, she often enviously watched the activity across the street, where love and contentment radiated like a light post in the neighborhood. More persuasive than a Norman Rockwell painting, her neighbor's place of grace got her attention, started a conversation, and eventually drew her to trust the love of Jesus.

Remember: Every time we open our front doors to receive others, we proclaim the gospel without saying a word. Grace is the widest door ever offered to make a stranger a friend.

Taste and See

I think there's something missing in our daily life—the joy of spontaneous visits. Honestly, I wish people would drop in more than they do. A simple glass of iced tea does great for a drop-in visit, but this Margarita Ice Cream Dessert is my favorite make-ahead recipe to keep in the freezer. It's easy, convenient, and the blend of creamy, sweet, and salty is out-of-this-world delicious. If the dessert is too tempting and you simply can't save it until someone pops in, invite a neighbor over or make a post on Facebook inviting the first person who responds to come over for this lime delight. This recipe would be perfect for a Christmas gathering.

Margarita Ice Cream Dessert

1¼ cup crushed pretzels
2 tablespoons sugar
⅓ cup butter, melted
½ gallon vanilla ice cream
One 10-ounce can frozen margarita concentrate
½ jar Dickinson's lime curd

Combine pretzels, sugar, and butter, reserving 2 tablespoons for topping. Press into bottom of 9-inch springform pan. Bake in preheated oven 375°F 8–10 minutes. Cool. In large bowl, soften ice cream and add margarita concentrate. Mix thoroughly. Put ice cream mixture in pan. Freeze until almost hardened. Carefully swirl lime curd into the ice cream with a knife. Sprinkle remaining pretzel mixture on top. Freeze. (Optional: Decorate with lime twists or strawberries.)

Daily Bread

"For the kingdom of God is not a matter of what we eat or drink, but of living a life of goodness and peace and joy in the Holy Spirit." (Romans 14:17 *NLT*)

Prayer

Jesus, may all who eat at my table find it to be a place of grace. Amen.

Altar Call

Savoring the presence of Jesus at your table creates a heart that loves to share the Good News.

CHAPTER 8

The Splendid Tastes of Heaven

Jesus the promise keeper anticipates serving meals in heaven.

"IT WILL BE GOOD
FOR THOSE SERVANTS
WHOSE MASTER FINDS
THEM WATCHING
WHEN HE COMES.
I TELL YOU THE TRUTH,
HE WILL DRESS HIMSELF
TO SERVE, WILL HAVE
THEM RECLINE AT THE
TABLE AND WILL COME
AND WAIT ON THEM."

(Luke 12:37)

The Jesus Table

Before we look at what Jesus has promised for our table experience in heaven, I want to tell you about one of his followers—my dad. I grew up in a home with a Saturday-morning ritual: pancakes cooked by Dad. I can still smell the cast-iron griddle heating up the corn oil my dad smeared on with a wadded paper towel. Dad had a rhythmic knack for whipping the Bisquick lumps into a smooth, creamy pool of batter. Before tipping a ladleful onto the griddle, he tested its temperature by flicking water droplets with his fingertips. The sizzle filled our ears with anticipation that the golden rounds would soon be on our plates.

Like a chef, Dad supervised every pancake, watching the bubbling batter bloom and pop. Feeding six kids pancakes must have tested his patience. It seemed as if he poured and flipped for a good hour. As a child, I just thought that's what dads do—they make yummy pancakes. Now looking back, I recognize this as the servant life of Jesus. Dad always fed us first. We never thought to say, "Oh, Dad, you need to have a pancake." After we mopped up the last bites on our syrup-sticky plates, he'd serve Mom, and if he were lucky, he'd get a pancake, too. Then he shined the cooled griddle before leaving the house to work on his Sunday sermons.

My childish heart didn't think about the distractions and responsibilities of his day; I just knew he cheerfully served us.

Dad's Saturday pancake ritual was one of his best sermons. Not only did he model servanthood, his faithful presence assured me I could always count on him. I knew I could always expect pancakes on Saturday. More importantly, I knew I could always expect to receive his love. I felt secure. This simple, profound assurance is what Jesus teaches when he talks to the disciples about the experience of the table in heaven.

Someday heaven and earth will be one. Jesus' death and resurrection assures us the new heaven and earth will come at the Father's appointed time. God's new creation will be an endless outpouring of his glory and our happiness. Our joy will revolve around Jesus and the benefits of feeling secure in his loving family. God's grace wins forever, and Saturday pancakes prepared by my dad gave me hints of eternity. As a teacher, Jesus always tied our here-and-now lives to the real life that is to come, and that is what Jesus also does in the conversation with his disciples recorded in Luke 12:35.

Just before promising to serve his followers meals in heaven, Jesus reminded the disciples that his Father's eyes see the tiny sparrow, the raven, and lilies of the field. This assurance calms our fears, but also encourages our faith, because those who trust Christ for their earthly needs and concerns have a place prepared at the Father's family table in heaven.

After giving these assurances, Jesus said, "Be dressed ready for service and keep your lamps burning. Like men waiting for their master to return from a wedding banquet, so that when he comes and knocks they can immediately open the door for him. It will be good for those servants whose master finds them watching when he comes. I tell you the truth, he will dress himself to serve, will have them recline at the table and will come and wait on them." (Luke 12:35–37)

"I tell you the truth." These words by Jesus mean, "This is really, really true! It matters to me, and it's going to happen! I am going to serve you!" Jesus wants us to *anticipate* the delights of glorified table life in heaven. When Jesus serves us, we will eat meals together knowing we're fully loved by and secure in the Father. We'll come to the table without pride, fear, competition, selfishness, fatigue, worry, or shame. All sin will be gone forever. And we'll look across our tables, appreciating the depth and beauty of Christ's life displayed in our brothers and sisters. Conversation will be rich and rewarding, and we will eat sensational food grown out of the new earth.

Jesus clearly implies that our faithful obedience (watchfulness) today ignites our anticipation of his promise to serve us. As far as Jesus is concerned, his promise of heaven's finest food served by the King of Kings, combined with perfect fellowship, ought to be one of the greatest motivations for being faithful.

Keep in mind that in this passage recorded in the gospel of Luke, Jesus wasn't referring exclusively to the marriage supper of the Lamb. That celebration (which will probably last for days) will occur before the Lord restores the new heaven and earth. I remember our daughters' engagements, the giddy searches for the perfect gowns, and the countdowns to their wedding days. The vows and feasting filled us with happiness. Yet these joys will be a faint whisper compared to the bliss that will someday be ours as the purified bride, united with the perfect groom.

After a wedding comes the life of marriage, and this is the context in which Jesus says he will serve us a meal. I don't understand the dimensions and logistics of heaven; we have to wait to see how Jesus will do this. And his promise to serve

Food will be what it was in Eden—a pure gift that magnifies the presence and goodness of God.

us doesn't mean we'll never creatively prepare and serve meals for our friends. But what we do know is this: Everything we do in the new heaven and earth will be joyful worship, magnifying God. We'll glorify God as we rule and play, explore and discover, create and love. And we'll live in homes. We'll have an address, a front door (with no lock), and, of course, a table for meals.

References to our table life in heaven are found in both the Old and New Testaments. Jesus certainly knew Isaiah's prophecy about the new heaven and earth: "They will build houses and dwell in them; they will plant vineyards and eat their fruit." (Isaiah 65:21) Glimpses of deep, authentic relationships and precious reunions in heaven show up in Jesus' many post-Resurrection meals, including the fish and bread cooked over an open fire just for Peter, who had denied the Lord. This activity, along with many scripture references to eating and feasting in the new kingdom, persuades me to believe that when I have my glorified body, I'll feast with God's family in perfect community. My redeemed taste buds will relish the fruits of the new earth, and Jesus will serve me. Food will be what it was in Eden—a pure gift that magnifies the presence and goodness of God.

+ + + + + + + + + + + +

The memory of my Dad's breakfast provisions keep speaking love to me. In some ways, I treasure it more today than during those pajama-clad Saturday mornings. It's just that now I appreciate the glory of Dad's breakfast gift. He was the servant delivering God's loving supply to my empty plate. This humbles me. Heaven is seeing Jesus face to face in the security of his love with his family. And for what it's worth, I think there will be pancakes in paradise.

Finding Your Table

Finding our tables on earth requires us to live forward toward heaven. Do you anticipate heaven? Do you feed your mind with scriptural pictures of heaven? For much of my Christian life, I've neglected to think clearly about what the Bible tells us concerning heaven, including the experience of heavenly table life. I've believed in the promise of heaven, but yielded to my lazy ignorance of it. "We'll find out when we get there" tended to be my attitude.

But remember how Jesus commended the faith of children? Children use their marvelous imagination to enjoy the literal meaning of God's promises, including heaven. I've eavesdropped on children excitedly chattering about seeing Noah or Daniel in heaven, no different than if they were planning on meeting him at McDonald's for a soft-serve ice-cream cone. In contrast, I've deferred much of heaven to metaphor or mystery.

When we look closer, we learn that not every Bible passage about heaven has literal meaning, but much of it does, including the enjoyment of food and reunion with friends around the table. In his book *Heaven*, Randy Alcorn writes, "What we otherwise could not have known about Heaven, because we're unable to see it, God says he has revealed to us *through his Spirit*. God has explained to us what Heaven is like in inspired scripture. Not exhaustively, but accurately. God tells us about Heaven in his Word, not so we can shrug our shoulders and remain ignorant, but because he wants us to understand and anticipate what awaits us."[1]

We learn about heaven not only by reading scripture, but also by practicing table life now. Can you remember a time when you just didn't want to leave the table? It was a hint of heaven. Easter came just days after my friend Deb was diagnosed with MS. I knew the news wouldn't keep her gifted fingers from the piano

Can you remember a time when you just didn't want to leave the table? It was a hint of heaven.

on Resurrection Sunday, but I couldn't get her bad news out of my mind. I called to invite her family for dinner, but they already had a guest list and a spiral honey-glazed ham chilling in their refrigerator, so we joined them instead. This was such a memorable experience that when I wrote a note of thanks, I made a copy of it for my own journal:

> *Sitting at your table this Easter was an extraordinary gift. After shouting and singing about our Lord's Resurrection, we came to your house to feast. There at your table, the old and the young, the weak and the strong, received yummy nourishment and storytelling laughter. We participated in all this* with you. *In the midst of your "heavy-news week," we lived* with you *the life of faith and hope. Your hospitality reflected the beauty of Christ's happiness. It was a treat, and we are blessed to know you as friends. We know that after Sunday comes Monday. We are praying for you both.*

Table life rings the dinner bell of hope. Fallen earth boasts of bad news, but we need to activate our memories to the rest of God's story. On that Easter afternoon in Deb's yellow house, the laughter and clear-eyed love poked holes through the threatening gray gloom of a serious diagnosis, and dinner was a vibrant taste of the promise of heaven.

Perhaps you've been like me—too detached from the significance of your table and heaven. On the other hand, you have probably heard the saying, "Don't be so heavenly minded that you're no earthly good." But table life is practical goodness preparing our heavenly reward. The older we get, the more likely we're inclined to think about heaven. When the psalmist wrote, "Teach us to number our days aright" (Psalms 90:12), he was asking God for a heart of wisdom to make every day count. Whether you are eighteen or eighty-eight, eternity is just around the corner. My friend Wes "plans" to live until he's ninety-five. Just the other day he showed me an app on his iPhone. It tells him how many days he has to live if he does reach ninety-five, and hospitality figures in as one of the important things to do in that remaining time.

When was the last time you said to yourself, "We've got to have so-and-so over for dinner" but didn't do it? Amazingly, when we share egg rolls or pot roast, it really does matter—for now and eternity. Every shared meal meets a need, provides a daily gift of joy, and points us to the pleasures of heaven. Take to heart the words of Jesus. Let him dismantle your ignorance and fortify your mouthwatering desires with splendid foretastes celebrated with the family of God. Your table will become an altar that invites you to eat with the kingdom identity that is yours forever.

Lifestyle Check: Do I make a habit of viewing the provisions of my table as reminders of the hope of heaven?

Heart Check: Is it difficult for me to accept that Jesus will serve me in heaven?

Setting Your Table

I'm no expert on heaven, but I know we'll have tables there. As you work at making your table on earth a splendid taste of heaven, do it with the following three perspectives that come straight from the heart of Jesus: security, reunion, and pleasure.

Security: Your table represents the security of being loved by Jesus forever. Your hospitality today is a tangible reminder of his promise to serve his children. It's a taste of heaven. The other day I got an e-mail from my friend Carolyn. She wrote, "What do you say to breakfast tomorrow on the deck? I know it's supposed to storm overnight, but it should be dry and warmer by morning. Let me know if that would work and what time you would like to eat. I am thinking poached eggs with tomatoes, arugula, smoked ham, Brie, and balsamic-Dijon reduction, along with coconut lattes. What do you think?" What do I think? *Yes! I'm coming over!* My first sip of the coconut latte was beyond delicious. But don't let Carolyn's flair for preparing a gourmet breakfast keep you from the main point of this story: Her hospitality celebrated God's love. I felt it.

Every meal is about God's love, but creating special meals that devote our attention to that love will enrich our lives. Christians set aside the table at Thanksgiving, Christmas, and Easter, but what about the other 362 days of the year? I think there will be more intentional feasting in heaven than there is now. It will be glorious, not gluttonous. Ancient Israel's calendar was packed with feast celebrations, and the early church had weekly love feasts. A love feast means just that—intentionally gathering to love one another. There was scripture, prayer, songs, and testimonies swirling around the potluck. Why not set a goal to celebrate one or two love feasts in your home? It could be to celebrate the birth of a child, dedicate a new home, commemorate a baptism, send your child off to college, or reminisce about a significant trip.

Reunion: My five siblings live from West Coast to East Coast. I miss them dearly and long for those happy times around the table. For some families, though, reunions are fraught with disappointment and conflict. But heaven will be a sweet reunion with every longing fulfilled and every disappointment banished. We will be reunited with Christ, our believing family, and believing friends. I've made many friends on earth whom I haven't yet met in person—people who have prayed for our family in times of trial, authors whose writings touched my life. I expect that in heaven I'll have dinner with them, enjoying their fellowship as I tell them how God used their prayers and words to touch my life.

We can use our tables now as a way of anticipating heaven's reunion. God made our senses of smell and taste exceptional memory banks, so why not prepare a favorite meal of a loved one who is now with Jesus? Let the aromas and tastes prompt a time for remembering and giving thanks. Whenever I brew some "Constant Comment" tea, I'm reminded of my mom sipping her afterdinner tea.

The four generations of my family gathered for a meal between the days of my father's burial and memorial service. On one of those days, we feasted on crunchy chips, carrot sticks, comforting soup, and an abundance of naughty desserts. Our tender, happy mayhem clustered around the kitchen and dining room all afternoon. It was enough food to last us a day. But I had come prepared to serve one more entrée. After a few hours passed, I took a poll: "Who will eat pancakes if I fix them?" Only three or four hands went up, but I wasn't thwarted. I turned on my sister-in-law's griddle, whipped up a modest batch of batter, and let the steamy aroma of Dad's specialty entice young and old. Even my beloved, wrinkled Mom ignored her diet protocol. The line got longer, the batches multiplied, and our indulgence was a happy tribute to Dad. And it was Saturday!

Pleasure: Have you noticed how heaven centers in food marketing schemes? As I stood refilling my three-gallon water jug at a store

Oh Dear!

My brother was anticipating Christmas and requested tacos for our extended family holiday dinner. Several days before Christmas, I purchased all the ingredients. But when I got out the ingredients to make our tacos on Christmas Day, I couldn't find the ground beef. I was so sure I'd bought several pounds for this occasion, searched both freezers and even the trunk of the car. The search was to no avail, so my son drove my husband in his SUV through the deep snow to several stores. But there were no stores open that sold ground beef. We improvised with chicken from our freezer. After seasoning, baking, and shredding the meat, dinner was served. We had a good laugh, made a new memory, and enjoyed the day and each other's company, which was the most important ingredient of all.

—Elaine

dispenser, a root beer display caught my eye. The beverage logo bragged, "So pure, you'll swear it's made in heaven." *M-m-m*, I'm tempted! Our heaven theology is Christ focused, not food focused, but enjoying palate pleasures with kindred hearts is our destiny.

Anticipating the marvelous food we will eat in heaven glorifies Jesus here on earth. Think back to a time you prepared a special dish. Didn't it please you to see your family or friends savor each bite? Jesus, who deserves all glory, will be glorified by our heavenly appetites delighting in every bite. I can't imagine a better peach than the vine-ripened peaches grown on the western slope of Colorado. Every August, we'd buy a case, rip the box open, and swoon over the sweet wonder of almost-perfect peaches. But the peaches Jesus will serve in the new earth will be sublime perfection.

The last food my frail father requested was coffee. He took a sip and then sent it back for a warm-up. His "picky" request was pure sweetness. Soon after this caffeine pleasure, he could only receive swabs of water placed in his mouth. As the life of his body began to fade, his soul fed off the manna of Christ alone. But someday his resurrected body will enjoy a slice of pecan pie with piping-hot coffee. And I'm going to be there to join him. Food is God's delicious gift to accentuate the blessing of being together as the family of God.

As we share our lives within the faith community, we see in one another how life brings suffering and pain, trials and tears. God's family is to be a haven of encouragement, hope, and healing. Little generosities are salve for the soul. Delicious food as simple as a basket of tangerines offers the refreshment of Christ's presence to the weary. When we share these gifts, we are trusting God to translate food's nourishment and pleasure for the body into strength for the soul.

Little generosities are salve for the soul. Delicious food as simple as a basket of tangerines offers the refreshment of Christ's presence to the weary.

Here's an idea on the fun side that highlights the pure pleasure of food: Host a "taste of heaven" meal where everyone brings their "to-die-for" dish. To add an element of surprise, don't assign the courses; just see what comes. While reveling in the delicious tastes, guide some table talk by asking your guests to share which Christ follower from history they especially wish to dine with in heaven. Jesus gives another fascinating heaven discourse in Luke 16:1–9. Alcorn's comments on this passage provide for much discussion around a meal: "Our friends in Heaven appear to be those whose lives we've touched on earth and who now have their own 'eternal dwellings.' Luke 16:9 seems to say these 'eternal dwellings' of our friends are places where we'll stay and enjoy companionship—second homes to us as we move about the Kingdom."[2]

Finally, anticipate the pure pleasure of food in heaven by exploring foods of other cultures. Distinctive foods are an inherent aspect of every culture, and all cultures will be redeemed by Jesus. Heaven on earth will be God's sovereign, global, international hallelujah. Jesus says, "I say to you that many will come from the east and the west, and will take their places at the feast with Abraham, Isaac and Jacob in the kingdom of heaven." (Matthew 8:11) There's going to be more than Americano fare of hamburgers and fries. Heaven will include glorious, satisfying international cuisine. As we enjoy fellowship with believers from every tribe and nation, we'll savor India's basmati rice, Puerto Rico's pigeon peas, Spain's paella, Libya's garbanzo lamb stew, France's chocolate mousse, Columbia's coffee beans, Serbia's stuffed peppers—and no antacids!

Go global now. Let God's plan for heaven open your eyes to your international neighbors, their tastes, and cultures. Step out on a gastronomical adventure, and as you do, you'll give respect to the people for whom Jesus died to bring to heaven.

The world is here, discover it! It's a taste of heaven. Recently, we ordered food from our favorite Thai restaurant, then brought it home for our Mother's Day family celebration. The cooks at the restaurant know we're their loyal fans. When I requested an extra portion of chicken in the *pra ram long song* dish, the owner said, "No charge for the extra. Happy Mother's Day!" His smile was the face of God's love. And dinner was fabulous. I'm looking forward to feasting with Thai believers in heaven, and I pray that the smiling restaurant owner will be there.

Is there a university or college near you? Find a way to get connected with international students and invite them to your home. As you share your food, ask about their country's cuisine, or give them free reign of your kitchen to prepare a meal from their homeland. But first take them to the ethnic grocery store of their choice and offer to pay the bill (since most college students are broke).

Eternity with Jesus Christ can be celebrated every time we come to the table. Believers anticipate heaven by setting the table with informed minds, open hearts of faith, and hands of love. Be watchful. Wait for heaven on earth by serving others a cup of water in Jesus' name.

Taste and See

We don't know exactly when Jesus will come back to bring to heaven his bride, the church, but his promise of love is every believer's hope. One of the most requested recipes from my kitchen is the beverage we served at both our daughters' weddings. Whatever joyful celebration you host, consider using this refreshing drink.

Wedding Punch Slush

1 small frozen can orange juice
1 small frozen can lemonade
1 teaspoon vanilla
1 teaspoon almond extract
¾ cups sugar
9 cups water
1 liter Sprite or ginger ale (for less sugar, use diet varieties)

Combine all ingredients but Sprite or ginger ale. Freeze until it's slushy. Add Sprite or ginger ale. Note: If you freeze the punch solid, thaw to a slush before serving. Makes 25 small servings.

Daily Bread

"In your presence is fullness of joy, at your right hand are pleasures forever more." (Psalms 16:11)

Prayer

Jesus, with humility I treasure your promise of serving a meal to me in heaven. May my table today portray the security of your love, the hope of sweet reunions, and the delight of food pleasures. All glory belongs to you forever. Amen.

Altar Call

Savoring the presence of Jesus at your table creates a heart that anticipates heaven.

CHAPTER 9

No Place Like Home—Yours!

Jesus the Lord wants to live at your table.

After my birth, my parents brought me home to a postwar stucco house on Juanita Avenue in Mill Valley, California. I was child number four, with two more to come. I shared a bedroom with my older sister, Martha; Mom and Dad slept on the hide-a-bed; and the plaster walls housed the woes and wonders of the Jones family. We lived there.

We afflicted our parents with sibling rivalry and clanking piano practice. Countless batches of chocolate chip cookies came from Mom's kitchen. We bathed, slept, played, disobeyed, learned to share, laughed, cried, and threw bread crust behind the refrigerator. Just weeks before my second birthday, this house sheltered my mother's pain as she sobbed in my father's arms after I had been hit by a truck speeding in the neighborhood.

Our family rituals were simple and few. Mom always put numbers—not names—on the Christmas packages. Rarely did our snooping outwit Mom's schemes. The narrow corner drawer in the kitchen was the depository for the NECCOs and M&M's reserved for our brown-bag lunches on Fridays. Looking back, I realize Friday featured a weekly blast of sugar highs, for not only did we get candy for lunch, but we also got a calculated six ounces of Pepsi with popcorn for an evening snack.

> "WHEN JESUS CAME BY, HE LOOKED UP AT ZACCHAEUS AND CALLED HIM BY NAME. 'ZACCHAEUS!' HE SAID. 'QUICK, COME DOWN! FOR I MUST BE A GUEST IN YOUR HOME TODAY.'"
>
> (Luke 19:5)

Our most common ritual, dinner at home, was functional, convenient, and economical—an apt description of 1950s households. But it was also so much more, not because dinner at the Jones house was ideal, but because it was sacred. That is, my parents had given their household to Christ. Their living faith honored the presence of Christ in their stucco bungalow. As children, we were unconscious of how their priorities would shape our souls, but the unseen guest lived among us.

I've salvaged one photograph of a family meal during those stucco house days. I'm sitting in a highchair, grasping a fork in my left hand (a true predictor of my handedness today). Set on the table are colorful metal cups, a fish-bowl-shaped water pitcher, and meat and potatoes. Dad is leaning in to coax us to smile at the camera. Of course, I have no recollection of the food or conversation. It looks as if it was a Sunday meal, and Dad probably couldn't wait for his afternoon snooze. But this photo tells me the story that there's no place like home when Jesus is honored there.

It was during our Mill Valley days that I heard the Bible story about Zacchaeus. I loved singing about the wee little man squatting in the branches of a sycamore tree, looking for Jesus in the crowd below. My Sunday school class sang the first stanza softly to mimic Zacchaeus as a wimpy little guy, then we boomed Jesus' command with a shout: "Zacchaeus, you come down! For I'm going to your house today!" The scene in that Jericho tree limb was as real as a Kodak image in my mind as I wiggled with the shout.

Though decades have passed since my Sunday school days, this gospel story keeps unfolding the centrality of the *place* of home in Jesus' ministry. I believe that if the Jericho sycamore tree had been Zacchaeus's actual residence, the Lord would have climbed right up there, too. But Zacchaeus did have a home, and Jesus knew the divine necessity of going to it. Homing in on Zacchaeus's heart meant going to his house. Let's imaginatively get inside Zacchaeus's mind on that day. Tell us your Jesus story, Zach:

I used to climb trees as a boy. I was nimble and fast, like a gymnast, but I hadn't climbed a tree in years. I was too busy climbing Herod's ladder as a tax-robbing crook. I didn't know Jesus, but when I saw the commotion around him, curiosity compelled me to hoist myself onto trunk and limb. Steadying myself for a good look, I was hoping not to be seen, but his unexpected gaze stunned me. I felt caught until he offered a way of escape. His insistence that we go to my house was a welcomed solution for my undignified perch. At least, that's how it felt to me.

I immediately jumped down. We jostled through the crowd, and as we walked together, I sensed he knew where I lived. His steps were lively and purposeful. I had plenty of enemies in Jericho, so people usually passed by my property with a sneer. But Jesus was different, and I welcomed him gladly. I gave him a cup of water while my wife told the servants to prepare a meal. As Jesus refreshed himself, I felt self-conscious about my lavish home and wondered if he had ever been in a house like mine. As minutes passed, I began to feel like a stranger in my own home. I squirmed and nervously chatted about nothing until it was time to eat.

When we sat down at the table, Jesus asked if he could bless the meal. I shrugged, obliging him with a sweaty nod. As he prayed while holding the bread, my eyes roamed my luxurious house once more; it haunted me. I knew my sin like the back of my hand. His gratitude for the food at my table mystified me— how could he bless a meal I had stolen? For years I used my house to hide from those who hated me, but here I heard Jesus thank God for the lamb chops from my kitchen. I felt a strange mingling of conviction and hope.

From that point on, Jesus was the host of the meal and forgiveness of sin was the topic of conversation; he wouldn't let it go. We sat at the table for hours until the time came for an unforgettable silent pause. The splendor in his eyes broke me.

Home is God's idea.

I fell at his feet to confess my sin and felt clean for the first time. Divine grace washed me. I can't explain it—it just happened. With my eyes locked on Jesus, I got up and promised to give half my possessions to the poor and pay back four times over those I had cheated. It seemed as if every corner of my house was purged by the breath of God. Then Jesus stepped closer to me, like a loyal friend eager to tell me something. I'll never forget what he said: "Today is salvation day in this home! Here he is, Zacchaeus, son of Abraham! For the son of man came to find and restore the lost." (Luke 19:9)

I was speechless. Like a birth announcement spoken by a proud father, his words confirmed I wasn't just a new person, I was a new son. I was home for the first time.

✦ ✦ ✦ ✦ ✦ ✦ ✦ ✦ ✦ ✦ ✦ ✦ ✦ ✦

Zacchaeus reminds us that God's kingdom disrupts our lives as it makes us whole. It changes everything, including our space called home. I've wondered how Mrs. Z. responded to her husband's decision to give away half their possessions. Talk about a home makeover! Imagine the table talk at breakfast the next day. Zacchaeus's new birth turned on a light inside his home, illuminating the stewardship of everything under his roof. It likely took time for Zacchaeus to work through the implications. But there's a liberating truth inside this redemption story: Jesus never condemned Zacchaeus's house as a vain possession. His house became more valuable, actually, because God had come to it; now it belonged to his kingdom. The house that was once a hollow monument to greed was now filled with gratitude. The house that was once a place to hide was transformed by a true confession. And the house that cornered an alienated man became the place where love restored him as a son. The Lord's living presence remade house and home.

God is Spirit, but Christ's insistence on going to Zacchaeus's house tells us that the tangible world of *place* matters to God. Home is God's idea. Even when Jesus spoke about heaven, he said, "Do not let your hearts be troubled. Trust in God, trust also in me. In my Father's house are many rooms; if it were not so I would have told you. I am going there to prepare a place for you. And if I go and prepare a place for you, I will come back and take you to be with me that you also may be where I am." (John 14:2–3)

I've never forgotten my primary-school grammar lesson on the definition of a noun—"a person, place, or thing." Home is person and place and thing, all wrapped as one unique gift. If I say, "I'm going to Eva's house," I'm letting you know I'm going to the geographical location where she lives (place), and I'll walk into the physical building of her house (thing) in order to be with my friend Eva (person).

Perhaps you've heard the saying, "If you want to see me, come anytime. If you want to see my house, make an appointment." This lighthearted wisdom underscores the importance of our human relationships, but also the "importance" of avoiding the blushing embarrassment of a drop-in guest seeing the wrinkled stack of laundry on the couch. But as the giver of every good and perfect gift, sometimes God wants us to open our front doors despite the unfinished work. Your house, condo, or studio apartment is not *just* wood, hay, and stubble. Though it can tragically burn, collapse, or blow away, it's a *place* for family life and kingdom life for as long as you are living there. Sadly for many, though, "Houses are the place we stage the life we wish we had time to live."[1]

Oh Dear!

It's interesting how parents influence your life long after they are gone. When I was about twelve years old an event happened at Sunday afternoon dinner that epitomized Mom's "grace under hospitality fire." The men were talking in the living room, other children were playing somewhere, and I was hanging around the fringes of the kitchen with several women. When it was about time to serve the meal Mom asked me to get the Jello salad ready. I was supposed to cut it into squares and put them on lettuce leaves. As I took the large glass dish to the table I dropped it upside-down on the floor in full view of everyone in the kitchen.

The most amazing outcome of that hospitality disaster was that Mom didn't yell at me or act like I had just ruined the dinner for the guests. I felt covered by her love and calm. It must have taken several minutes to clean up the sticky slick mess imbedded with broken glass. It could have been a wounding memory for me if Mom had responded with words of shame.

I don't remember that anyone missed the Jello salad that afternoon. And we probably had a delicious dessert that made up for it! As a young girl I was eternally grateful for Mom's response. She taught me what's important in the "big" picture and that I was more important than Jello.

—Karen

As with Zacchaeus, as with all believers, Christ's declaration of "I'm coming to your house today" translates into daily reality. Our hearts are his dwelling place, and our homes are his sacred space. He's there. God is with us when we're putting the groceries away, looking for a toothpick, or writing a letter. Every room matters to God. I once stood in my kitchen, opening an envelope from my grandson, who had sent me a handmade birthday card. I, the privileged recipient of his first colored drawing on his gargantuan new paper, reveled in his gift. The masterpiece required several magnets to hold it securely on my refrigerator door. Then I stepped back and smiled. I felt pleasure knowing Christ was sharing the moment with me. He delighted in the picture on my refrigerator, too.

Sometimes the familiar veils the fantastic. Are you so accustomed to or disgruntled with the spaces and routines of your home that you neglect to treasure Christ's actual presence? He is there, but do you notice? Sometimes practicing hospitality can reacquaint you to your own home. When we gather friends in our homes, the happy chatter fills it with energy. And when they leave, the quiet is an opportunity to reflect upon the gifts Christ gave in the fellowship. He is there, waiting for our remembering of what he has done.

Your home is as unique as your personality, and no matter what your home is like, Christ lives there. There's no "one-home-fits-all" house plan in God's kingdom. I've been in a bullet-battered apartment in Bosnia, a mountain manse in Colorado, and a chicken-coop house in Croatia. Each one holds distinct memories of people—their stories, their passions, their faith. Their stories have become part of my story. The simple, poor house Jesus grew up in was profoundly different from Zacchaeus's lavish Jericho house, but God's presence filled both. Both homes were needed to glorify God on earth. So is yours.

Author Christine Pohl writes, "The most potent setting for hospitality is in the overlap of the private and public space. It flourishes at the intersection of the personal intimate characteristics of home and the transforming expectations of the church."[2] So ask yourself this question: *Does the couple who often sits behind you in church know just the back of your head, or have they discovered your interest in history, art, or gardening by being in your home?* Welcoming churches and welcoming homes give glory to our welcoming God.

A vital sign of vibrant church life is when it mirrors the natural yearnings of kindred love. I want to be with those I love *where* they live. It gives me a gift— being in their homes helps me carry them in my heart when I leave. And vice versa. When our grandkids visit, it's fun to take them to McDonald's for an indulgence of junk food, but I can't imagine them never sitting at our table or helping me make cinnamon rolls in my kitchen. McDonald's is neutral space; home is personal space. It's as true with our immediate families as it is with our church families.

Though hospitality is occasional, it's powerful. In *Practicing the Presence of People*, Mike Mason writes: "Becoming a Christian begins with recognizing God in one human being, Jesus Christ, and goes on to the recognition of God's image in every other person."[3] When you invite someone to your home for a meal, it says,

You home is as unique as your personality and no matter what your home is like, Christ lives there.

"I noticed you. I'm thinking of you. I want to share my personal space with you." What superb gifts! Even if he can't come, he'll remember the invitation.

Refresh your focus on your home with the footprint of the Zacchaeus story. Begin by cherishing the memory of the glad welcome you yourself received from God on the day of your new birth. It probably didn't begin on a tree limb, but eventually you ended up at home. Go ahead—walk through your front door. Leave the virtual world, and enter the *real* world of home. Oops—watch out for the shoes piled in the doorway! Drop the junk mail on the counter. Resist turning on your iPod. You've got five minutes until your grass-stained son drags home, cranky and hungry. Sit in your favorite chair, and ask God to make known your unseen guest.

If your heart or home feels in disarray today, remember God is the faithful restorer of your dwelling place. God knows what kind of day you've just had. Did you lose your temper or steal someone's reputation by gossiping? Let the roof over your head remind you of the security of the Father's forgiveness. "When we were overwhelmed by sins, you forgave our transgressions. Blessed are those you choose and bring near to live in your courts! We are filled with good things of your house, of your holy temple." (Psalms 65:3–4)

Home isn't really home if we hide who we are. Are you so exhausted from futile attempts to please everyone that you feel like a fake? Are you longing for the comfort of your ragtag pajamas or a therapeutic scream into your pillow? Let the windows of home remind you that God's saving light promises the wholeness of your new self in Christ. "How great the love the Father has lavished on us, that we should be called children of God. And that is what we are!"(1 John 3:1)

Do you need a renewal of God's love today? Recall the simple ways love has lived in your house—hugs in the hallway, bedtime backrubs, kind words saved on the answering machine. Cherish these memories as you open your heart to the intimate fellowship of Christ. Acknowledge that the Lord treasures your table, so dedicate it as a place to celebrate the company of Christ. Sit there—nibble a pretzel, peel an orange, or sip some Chai tea. Humbly receive from Christ these little magnificent gifts of love. "Because your love is better than life, my lips will glorify you...My soul will be satisfied as with the richest of foods." (Psalms 63:3–5)

Throughout the biblical narrative, the table has begged lovers of God to center their ordinary days on the grace of the miraculous. Zacchaeus was just one of millions who has been surprised by grace. He left his house in the morning to go steal money; took a detour up a tree; then jumped down, not knowing he was jumping into the arms of God. His table became the place where he was transformed by love. God wrote the script, and Zacchaeus joined in.

The blessing Jesus probably spoke over every meal was a traditional Jewish prayer called the *berakoth*: "Blessed be thou, Lord God, King of the universe, who brings forth bread from the earth." Brings forth! The blessing announced the miraculous. On the Galilean hillside, Jesus began with five loaves of bread, and in the end, the disciples collected twelve extra batches of bread in laundry-size baskets after feeding thousands of hungry bellies. Jesus is still providing for us. Today, believers receive the miracle in order to share the miracle.

After Christ's Resurrection and Ascension, the early church grew as the Holy Spirit worked through two primary means—by proclaiming the gospel and by practicing hospitality. What a contrast this is to the pattern of our culture today, where bad news and unlived-in homes are often the norm. But Christian homes are countercultural. "As for me and my house, we will serve the Lord." (Joshua 24:15) When I walk through my neighborhood on a winter night, the unlit homes

Throughout the biblical narrative the table has begged lovers of God to center their ordinary days on the grace of the miraculous.

fade into icy darkness. But, oh, the beauty of a single lamp or candle illuminating a home. Hospitality illumines the world's darkness with a lifestyle transformed by the life of Jesus. His life is our example. Author Dallas Willard writes in *The Spirit of the Disciplines*, "We can, through faith and grace, become like Christ by practicing the types of activities he engaged in, by arranging our whole lives around the activities he himself practiced in order to remain constantly at home in the fellowship of his Father."[4] Table life isn't just about imitating Christ's hospitality; it's about experiencing the Father's love.

Taste and See

Here it is: The once-a-year favorite dinner entrée in the Thompson home. The true test of excellence is that our sons-in-law consume it. I guarantee you won't have any leftovers.

Grilled Pork Tenderloin with Port Wine Sauce

Meat and Marinade

6 pork tenderloins
¼ cup vermouth
4 tablespoons fresh thyme (or 2 teaspoons dried thyme)
1 teaspoon salt
1 tablespoon fresh minced garlic

Mix ingredients. Marinate pork overnight in refrigerator. On the next day, grill meat. Let "rest" a few minutes before slicing diagonally.

Sauce

One 750-milliliter bottle tawny port wine
1 tablespoon minced shallots
3 cups whipping cream
½ cup dried cranberries

This sauce is based on reduction, so it may take up to 3 hours to make. It is best to make the sauce just before serving meal, not the night before. In a saucepan, cook down the port and shallots until reduced to 2 cups. Add cream and cook until sauce thickens and almost caramelizes. Be patient! Add dried cranberries. Drizzle some sauce on the sliced meat, and put the remainder in a gravy bowl.

Daily Bread

"As for me and my house, we will serve the Lord." (Joshua 24:15b)

Prayer

Yes, Lord, my home is yours. Use it as you will. In Jesus' name, amen.

Altar Call

Savoring the presence of Jesus opens my front door.

Epilogue

The best stories are real-life stories. You are the storyteller. What stories about your home do you want to pass on to the next generation? Table life is no fairy tale; it's real, practical, and rewarding. It unites the here and now with eternity. And yet, it requires intention. I have one special recollection of walking through the back door of our kitchen to the garage, and it speaks to me the significance of a table and the place of home. This is what happened...

Our daughters, Jill and Shelly, grew up with the sounds of their dad's table saw ringing in their tender, pink ears. They usually avoided his sawdust cave, but the older they got, the more they admired his craftsmanship. They married handsome heroes, moved into their first apartments, and called home to ask if Dad would make some furniture. The day came when the request for a table became the project in the garage. Roger measured, cut, glued, planed, sanded, stained, and waxed Midwest cherry wood until he formed it into an elegant oblong dining room table. Then it stood lifeless in our garage. Weeks passed as we looked for a way to transport it from Minnesota to Texas.

Every time I took out the trash to the garbage can in the garage, I would walk past the table covered by a stiff brown drop cloth speckled with paint, dry wall mud, stain, and hardened globs of glue. It was an incongruent sight for my table life heart. The table is for the home, not the garage. But the time finally came for the table to hitchhike a ride on a moving van. It left our garage with Roger's name written underneath, along with a poem I wrote as a prayer of dedication. Days later, it arrived to its home, ready to be honored as the place to celebrate the hospitality of Christ.

Come to the Table

Cherry wood
once nourished,
by roots sipping
earth's extravagance,
exalts Christ's
pure and spacious call
"Come to the table!"

Esteemed by craftsman's hands,
a verdant splendor glows,
the table
serving
God's glad welcome
home.
He waits
to bless
and celebrate.

Stranger, friend, family,
Gather, Listen, Eat!
'round this molded gift
of time and space.
Heed not the world's distractions.
Give honor to this place.

Expect Christ's revelation.
Listen, Laugh, Love.
Tell your pilgrim stories
'round table manna
without cost.
Pray for one another.
Feast with joy.
His grace abounds
forevermore.

Discussion Questions

Chapter 1: Called to Table Life

Questions for Reflection or Discussion

1. How does it feel to remove the pressures of cooking like the stars?

2. What appeals to you about the cooking shows? Why?

3. Describe the table in your house now or when you were young. What story comes to mind?

4. What is one small goal you can do right now to improve table life in your home?

5. The author suggests "pressures of our culture and idols of our hearts" hinder and hide table life. What hindrances currently make table life difficult in your home?

6. How does viewing your table as an altar impact your idea of eating meals together?

Going Deeper

1. The power of table life is seen in the pages of the Old Testament. Read the following stories. Where do you see the themes of faith and joy? What transformation of heart happened at these tables?

   Jonathan and Mephibosheth (2 Samuel 9:1–2)

   Abraham and Sarah (Genesis 18:1–13)

   Elijah and Woman of Shulamith (1 Kings 17:7–24)

2. Take time to remember someone's table that has touched your life. It may have been last week or years ago. It might be the table of a parent or a mentor, a close friend, or a new acquaintance. Write that person a note expressing how that mealtime touched your life.

Chapter 2: Thanks for Supper, Mom!

Questions for Reflection or Discussion

1. If you could ask Mary, the mother of Jesus, one question about how she handled mealtime and its preparations, what would that question be?

2. What are the attitudes and habits of mealtime in your home right now? Describe both positives and negatives as concretely as you can.

3. Ask yourself, "What's one thing I can do to make meals special?"

4. How does your family cherish Sundays? How is it reflected in your Sunday meals?

5. What are ways you can foster a spirit of gratitude at the table?

6. "Mealtime is God's metronome designed to bind our busy lives to the Father." Our souls long for rhythm, yet it's often difficult to begin and/or maintain. What's one obstacle that tends to pull your family off balance?

7. Every yes simultaneously means many nos. Think of the things you are now saying yes to. What can you say no to in order to prioritize a yes to your family table?

Going Deeper

1. Take a twenty-minute coffee or tea break to meditate on Romans 12:1–2. One way to meditate is to slowly read the verse in several translations or paraphrases. Pray these verses as a prayer of commitment to pursue the rewards of table life with your family.

2. There are many faith treasures found in our Jewish roots that pertain to table life today. Explore some treasures, such as memorizing Deuteronomy 6:4–6; reading a book about Jewish feasts, such as *Celebrating Biblical Feasts* by Martha Zimmerman; or watch the Sabbath meal scene in the movie *Fiddler on the Roof.*

Chapter 3: A Timely Invitation

Questions for Reflection or Discussion

1. If Jesus in the flesh were to literally knock on your front door, what meal or snack would you most want to share, and why? What would you anticipate?

2. Do you think most women have a desire to be hospitable? Explain.

3. How does the commitment to "linger at the table" and "live in the moment" work together? What's the hardest part about living in the moment?

4. What is your stronger inclination within your local worshipping community—to be a giver or receiver? What is one step you need to take to more fully enjoy the reciprocal life?

5. If you are married, describe your most rewarding "doing it together" hospitality.

6. Sometimes we need to "laugh our way" to a new day. Describe a flop, disaster, or Murphy's Law dinner night that almost convinced you to never again do the hospitality thing.

7. Whose home would you like to be invited to, and why?

Going Deeper

1. Jesus said to his disciples, "He who receives you receives me, and he who receives me, receives the one who sent me." (Matthew 10:40) If you were to cultivate the habit of imagining you are receiving Christ when you receive others into your home, how do you think it would transform your attitude about hospitality?

2. Gratitude and humility are inseparable. Receiving and sharing daily bread is God's way of growing this fruit in our lives. The next time you make a grocery list, write on the other side the names of your family and someone you'd like to invite for dinner. Use this as a prompter to pray, asking God to use your table to grow humility and gratitude in his children.

Chapter 4: Surprise!

Questions for Reflection or Discussion

1. How is faith part of your table life?

2. What does it mean to you to "Practice the presence of God" at your table? How can you foster this attitude?

3. Can you think of a meal you especially remember as a divine appointment? Was it one you prepared or one you received from another?

4. Make a list of objects you might use to place at the center of your table to symbolize something meaningful to the Christian faith experience. How would you explain them to your guests, and what questions might you ask to stimulate conversation?

Going Deeper

1. Start a "Taste and See" hospitality journal. Record memories (even just one paragraph) of the fellowship experience, or write out a prayer of thanks for how you experienced Christ at the meal. You'll be amazed by how this fortifies your faith for years to come.

2. Find a "hospitality buddy"—someone who shares the faith vision of the table life you desire. Perhaps preparing a meal is easy for you, but you'd like your buddy to prepare questions and conversation topics. Do it together.

3. Purchase a cross or other wall art for your eating area that can serve as a daily reminder of Christ's presence.

Chapter 5: Don't Fuss

Questions for Reflection or Discussion

1. What do you most appreciate about Mary as well as Martha?

2. What one self-imposed standard of hospitality do you need to let go of?

3. Ask yourself, "When I have people to my home for a meal, is it mostly about God, me, or them?"

4. What is one aspect of your home that others enjoy? That you enjoy?

5. What one practical suggestion in this chapter is helpful to you? Explain why.

6. What's the difference between *caring* for your home versus *obsessing* about it?

7. When are you most likely to compare your home to others'?

Going Deeper

1. Identify some aspect of media you want to "fast" from for a season in order to enhance the freedom life of hospitality.

2. The struggle for identity is ubiquitous. The author suggests that being a "cooperative friend of Jesus" is an aspect of our Christian identity. How does this concept inspire you to practice hospitality differently?

Chapter 6: My Father's Glad Welcome

Questions for Reflection or Discussion

1. The joy of the father in the parable is revealed by his several flauntings of Jewish custom and protocol. Consider and comment on the significance of the father's actions.

2. Describe some characteristics of the table in the home of the prodigal son.

3. Recall and describe the emotions you felt when someone extended a glad welcome to you.

4. What is your reaction to the author's suggestion that hospitality might be used to bless the restoration of a once-broken relationship?

5. Do you think the elder brother eventually joined the dinner party? Has there ever been an event you refused to go to, but then later regretted your decision?

Going Deeper

1. Take time to remember your "glad welcome" reception into God's love. Spiritual maturity moves forward, reaches up, and grows deep roots; but there's power in returning to our first love. Read Revelations 2:4. How can a practice of hospitality fan into flame the joy of your "first love" encounter with Christ?

2. Do you currently have a broken relationship in the body of Christ? How does the picture of breaking bread with that person motivate or threaten you? Take time at your own table to pray for this relationship, asking God to give you the next step.

3. Is your heart struggling with a prodigal son or daughter? As you wait, weep, and pray, take time to boldly imagine the meal you would serve if that child were to return to the Father.

Chapter 7: A Place of Grace

Questions for Reflection or Discussion

1. Ask yourself, "What hesitations and fears do I have about having outsiders in my home?" In what ways does it feel risky to you?

2. Ask yourself, "How could God use my unique story to reach out to others?"

3. Several ideas expressed in this chapter are listed below. Personalize and comment on each one. Remember people God has brought into your life who have offered these gifts to you. How does their example inspire you?

> Noticing the need of the human heart.
>
> Hospitality is the happy overflow of a forgiven heart.
>
> Love your story and pass it on.

4. What does the word *haven* mean to you?

Going Deeper

1. Meditate on the attributes of the kingdom as described in Romans 14:17—"righteousness, peace, and joy in the Holy Spirit." What words would you pick to describe the opposites of these attributes, which we see destroying people and families today? Take time to ask God to make your house a place of peace and joy.

2. Find another believer in your neighborhood and plan together a root-beer-float block party. Make it an annual event, creating expectation and connection. This can build comfort zones and bridges to later invite neighbors inside your home for a meal or to respond in a time of need.

Chapter 8: The Splendid Tastes of Heaven

Questions for Reflection and Discussion

1. Keeping in mind the words *security*, *reunion*, and *pleasure*, what are two things you can do that would help reflect the hope of heaven at your table?

2. What's the strongest food you've ever tasted? What country's food would you like to try?

3. What meal- or food-related tradition do you have now or had growing up?

4. Choose one practical suggestion in this chapter that stretches you and is meaningful to you. Explain why.

5. Describe some attributes of the table we will enjoy in heaven.

Going Deeper

1. How does letting others serve you now prepare your heart for the time when Jesus will serve you in heaven?

2. The next time you eat a particularly delicious meal, take time to write Jesus a letter of thanks, expressing your anticipation of heaven to come.

3. Delayed gratification intensifies our longings. Just as we wait for heaven, many in the world are waiting for a meal. Serve your family just rice once a week for a month. Use the table time to remember the needs of the hungry in prayer. Donate to a food shelf or other ministry the money you saved by just eating rice.

4. Meditate on Revelations 19:9: "Blessed are those who are invited to the wedding supper of the Lamb!" Whose salvation are you praying for?

Chapter 9: No Place Like Home—Yours!

Questions for Reflection or Discussion

1. If you were Zacchaeus's wife, how do you think you would have responded to the events of the day?

2. What does the following quote mean to you: "Homing in on his heart meant going to his house"?

3. In what simple ways does love live at your house? What room in your house needs to be transformed from being "staged" to being "lived in"?

4. Describe your favorite place in your home to meet with God. Think of the times God's grace and love have blessed you there. Pray that those intimate moments with God will become like a scent diffuser that spreads a fragrance through the rest of the house.

4. If a family member were to walk through your home after you are gone, what artifact would she pick as a symbol of your life at home?

Going Deeper

1. "As for me and my house, we will serve the LORD" has been printed on plaques for decades. Do a "prayer walk" through your home. Or plan a dinner party to dedicate your house to the Lord. Involve your children. Share the occasion with a few friends.

2. "The table has begged lovers of God to center their ordinary days with the grace of the miraculous." Every house holds memories. Select an annual date when you set goals for making your table a place for celebrating the grace of the miraculous.

3. Rent the film *Babette's Feast.* It's a Danish film (so it has subtitles), but it's a fascinating story about how a table transforms relationships. It's slow moving, but worth the viewing and some conversation with friends.

Notes

Chapter 1: Called to Table Life

1. Ken Gire, *The Reflective Life* (Colorado: Chariot Victor, 1998), 11.

Chapter 2: Thanks for Supper, Mom!

1. William J. Doherty, PhD and Barbara Z. Carlson, *Putting Families First* (New York: Henry Holt, 2002), 9.

2. Ibid, 5.

3. Joetta Handrich Schlabach, *Extending the Table* (Pennsylvania: Herald Press, 1991), 202.

4. Paul Tournier, *The Meaning of Gifts* (Virginia: John Knox Press, 1973), 6.

5. William Doherty and Barbara Z. Carlson, *Putting Families First* (New York: Henry Holt, 2002), 119.

6. Melodie Beattie, book source unknown.

Chapter 3: A Timely Invitation

1. Edith Schaffer, *What Is A Family?* (New Jersey: Fleming Revel, 1997), 211.

Chapter 4: Surprise!

1. Alexander Strauch, *The Hospitality Commands*, (Colorado: Lewis & Roth, 1993), 35.

2. Marilyn McEntyre, "Care of The Word" *Westmont* magazine, fall 2007, 12.

Chapter 5: Don't Fuss

1. Sharon Hersh, *Bravehearts* (Colorado: WaterBrook Press, 2000), 78.

Chapter 7: A Place of Grace

1. Craig L. Blomberg, *Contagious Holiness* (Illinois: InterVarsity Press, 2005), 130.

2. John Piper, *The Passion of Jesus Christ* (Illinois: Crossway, 2004), 104.

Chapter 8: The Splendid Tastes of Heaven

1. Randy Alcorn, *Heaven* (Illinois: Tyndale, 2004), 19.

2. Ibid, 323.

Chapter 9: No Place Like Home—Yours!

1. Marjorie Garber, magazine source unknown.

2. Christine Pohl, *Making Room* (Michigan: Wm. B. Eerdmans, 1999).

3. Mike Mason, *Practicing the Presence of People* (Colorado: WaterBrook Press, 1999), 21.

4. Dallas Willard, *The Spirit of the Disciplines* (New York: HarperCollins, 1991), ix.